"Dr. Ryan Bentley practices what he preaches. This book is not only a reflection of an intense study of what makes the body work from a biblical and scientific view; it's also a personal reflection of his own commitment to living healthy and whole. Want a better, more thriving life? Read it!!"

—Dan Seaborn, Founder of Winning At Home, Inc.

"An amazingly insightful book for Christians to truly understand and genuinely live the message of 'body as temple.' Dr. Bentley's guiding, bright light of grace and wisdom artfully combines faith and food, belief and biology, healing and health in a way to help people effect positive change in their lives, from the chronically ill to the walking wounded. He is the ultimate guide to congruent, authentic living of body, mind, and spirit. With clarity and ease, Dr. Bentley walks the talk, and through his example and written word he inspires the uninspired and informs the uninformed in a powerful, loving way, unlike any other physician. He is the 'Rick Warren of modern medicine'!"

—Deanna Minich, PhD, FACN, CNS, nutritionist and author

"Dr Bentley was able to weave our spiritual and physical well-being in a sweeping panorama that encompasses a world of mind and physical exercise and healthy eating. He has made a compelling case for our 'duty' to take care of our bodies. After reading this wonderful book, no Christian can ever again dissociate his or her physical being from his or her spiritual journey. Kudos."

—Souheil F. Haddad, MD

"This book by Dr. Ryan Bentley is one of the greatest books I've ever read. It covers every aspect of life, from love, medicine, and health to our Lord and Savior Jesus Christ. Tying all of these aspects into one book is brilliant. I truly believe this book has it all and is a must-read!"

—Craig Bowden, PGA tour golfer

"To treat the entire person, neither the doctor nor the patient can ignore their spiritual health and how it reflects in the physical person. I will be recommending this book to every patient. Once again a unique look at truth, Dr. Bentley style."

—Shawn Benzinger, DC, DACBO, FIAMA

"Ryan talks about 'health, healing and faith—and how they all fit together.' They do indeed fit together very well. In fact, the 'fit' is far greater than most doctors, personal trainers, and church pastors understand or publicly recognize. That is why Ryan's book is right on target and why I'm excited about it. Ryan brings passion to the dialog around intertwining physical and spiritual fitness. He helps readers thrive. I particularly like his chapter on boundaries. He challenges readers to consider how they are enslaved to their gifts and how 'comfortable' creates a separation in our relationship with God. *Ouch!* There is no feel-good message here. Instead, Ryan talks about movement, not just physically and spiritually but also in unexpected ways. That is the real *aha* of this book, to read and then discover the personal purpose God has just for you. Ryan wants to help you discover how to fulfill God's good purpose and be a vessel continually and generously overflowing to others. This is a fitness book bound to move you to be life to others."

—Brad Bloom, Publisher, *Faith & Fitness Magazine*, faithandfitness.net

"This book uses Jesus Christ's teachings to explain how we can be inspired to be healthy forever."

—Anup Kanodia, MD, MPH

Dr. Ryan E. Bentley

Vessels that Thrive

Choosing a Lifestyle of
Health, Healing, and Faith

ISBN: 978-1-935391-89-0

Cover design by Frank Gutbrod
Interior design and composition by Frank Gutbrod
Editing by Paul J. Brinkerhoff
Printed in the United States of America
First Edition

To my great friend Richard Hogsett and to a man
whom I never personally met, Joe Hamm, both of whose sudden
and tragic departures from their time here on earth
have sent me and my family into a deeper understanding
of what it truly means to be walking by faith,
fulfilling our purpose, and focusing on being present in every
moment, for one never knows which one may be our last.

We are forever grateful for the impact you have made
on our family's life. God bless you and your legacy
for the generations to come.

"The doctor of the future will give no medicine but will interest his patients in the care of the human frame, in diet and in the cause and prevention of disease."
Thomas Edison

"Who needs a doctor: the healthy or the sick? I'm here inviting outsiders, not insiders—an invitation to a changed life, changed inside and out."
Jesus of Nazareth

Contents

Introduction

*"Out of all the voices calling out to me I will choose
to listen and believe the voice of truth."*
Casting Crowns

*"And you will know the truth,
and the truth will set you free."*
John 8:23 (NLT)

Early in my practice of guiding people towards health, a patient said to me, "I guess I am not sick enough yet to make the lifestyle changes you ask of me, but I will be back when I am." I was speechless. I could not understand why she did not value herself, her life, and her purpose enough to take care of her body. After all, we only have one body and one life to live on earth.

As time went on, I realized that many of my patients felt this same way. Although they may not have spoken it directly to me, their actions most certainly demonstrated the same attitude as the woman who did admit her crippling belief. Apparently, physicians aren't the only ones encountering this values set and its accompanying attitude toward health among those whom they seek to serve. A Christian theologian shared a similar exchange that occurred in his office one day while talking with one of his seminary students.

Early in my career of teaching systematic theology, a student arranged an appointment with me in my office. After the customary small talk, he cut to the quick: He was experiencing multiple physical problems, plagued by insomnia, digestive and excretory problems, blood in his urine, lethargy, and attention deficit. He wondered what spiritual causes could lie at the heart of these physical symptoms, and he wanted my advice about how to become well again. I hardly needed to probe much, but my questions caught him off guard because they focused on physical matters: What are you eating? (junk food) Are you scheduling rest periods? (Too busy for relaxation) How are you exercising? (No need for that) Becoming irritated with my line of questioning, he offered the following: Because his body was going to be sloughed off at death anyway, he did not need to be concerned about eating well, resting well, and exercising well.

I countered with an observation: His body was (literally) breaking down before his eyes, and he would soon be no good for himself, his family, and the church ministry for which he was preparing through his seminary studies. And, I added, I thought the problem was a physical one, not a spiritual one. But that was not the answer a "spiritually minded" evangelical like him was accustomed to hearing. Besides, this student had come to me with an expectation that I would share something with him from the Word of God. But I was not prepared to do so.

This encounter plunged me into a crisis: As a professor of theology at an evangelical seminary, I wondered what I should have shared with this student from Scripture that would have helped him with his physical problems. If you found yourself in a similar situation, what would you communicate?[1]

What a great question! Do physical problems suggest spiritual issues that need to be addressed and resolved as well? In a postmodern world where the "spiritual" is in, few people deny any more the mind-body connection. Sometimes our ailments are perhaps more a question of mind over matter, or mind moving matter. If we lack self-discipline in the physical aspects of life, does that tend to affect our spiritual endeavors, even the practice of spiritual disciplines? In the course of this book, I will make an effort to offer an answer to the question of what I could have communicated to my patient or the professor to the seminary student by propose a functional approach to this question, both in terms of the physical and of the spiritual aspects of our health problems. Although I am writing as a Christian who is a practicing health provider, I am writing not only to those whose primary allegiance in life is to the Lord Jesus Christ but also to those who are not (yet) followers of Jesus Christ but who may be looking for answers to questions they have about their health or healing or faith and how they all fit together. So let's get started!

Truth and Lies

I believe the conversation with my patient and this professor's interview with his student both highlight the avoidance of truth. Our culture and its broken healthcare system have programed us to believe that to make a change we first have to be sick, instead of being healthy to avoid being sick. I prayed for God to reveal to me how to help inspire people to value God's workmanship (our bodies) enough to take proper care of the body they have been blessed with, so they can live life in accordance with God's good purpose.

Since then, God has opened my eyes to the fact that a large percentage of the church of Jesus Christ lives in a way that looks exactly like that of people who do not have the Holy Spirit of God living in them. Does not God's Word teach us that we are called to stand out from the crowd and be different from the surrounding culture? Are these suggestions to consider or commands to obey?: "Offer your bodies as living sacrifices, holy and pleasing to God—this is your spiritual act of worship [or reasonable service]. Do not conform any longer to the pattern of this world, but be transformed by the renewing of your mind" (Rom. 12:1–2). But much of what we believe to be true is often based more on comforts and pleasures of this world than on God's Word. This pursuit of worldly comfort displaces many believers from a fully aligned life with the Holy Spirit.

Do you believe everything we hear or read is truthful, accurate, and helpful in shaping our beliefs? This is an important question to ask because our beliefs begin with the information we receive and accept as true. Every day we are presented with the opportunity to either blindly believe whatever we hear and read or to take the initiative to search for the truth as we would for hidden treasure. This is what the apostle Paul says Christians are able to do if they obey God by offering themselves in service to Him and undergo a transformation in their thinking by letting God's truth renew their minds by the working of God's Spirit: "Then you will be able to test and approve what God's will is—his good, pleasing and perfect will" (Rom. 12:2). It is this daily evaluation of the information being presented to us that determines what we choose to believe and ultimately who we become. With the ability to accurately discern between truth and deceit comes great responsibility, as our outcome in life is ultimately a culmination of our beliefs and choices.

Truth is what gives us a life that we are able to truly enjoy and live to the fullest. Unfortunately, we live in a culture where lies are often presented as truth, and if we are not careful to discern the difference we may unknowingly make decisions that have grave consequences. In general, we assume that what we choose to believe is fact. But have we really studied what we believe to be true, or do we believe something to be true simply because we are told it is?

As it pertains to health, or, more appropriately stated, the *lack* of health among our general population, it is apparent that many people have unknowingly bought in to the deceit of today's modern culture. I would like to see us create a new culture where *zero* of the top *ten* causes of death are related to poor lifestyle choices, as opposed to the current rate, where *seven* of the top *ten* causes of death relate to poor lifestyle choices.[2] John K. Iglehart, former editor of the journal *Health Affairs*, expressed the view of health promotion in the United

States that emphasizes people's individual behavior as a huge factor contributing to the health problems we face as a society.[3] Iglehart said,

> [M]ost illnesses and premature death are caused by human habits of living that people choose for themselves: alcohol and other drug abuse, tobacco smoking, nutritional preferences [i.e., the American diet], and reckless driving. . . . [N]early two-thirds of all illnesses and untimely deaths could have been prevented. . . . [C]hanging human behavior is the heart of the matter, and perhaps no challenge is greater in a society that so values free enterprise, individualism, and a limited role for its government in personal lives.[4]

We live in a society where media promotes fear, along with a culture that fosters instant gratification and quick fixes. Thus, today's culture has created a cycle of fear and instant gratification that is unhealthy and ultimately unfulfilling. Advertisers and the mainstream media play on our emotions in an effort to influence how we think, the food choices we make, and our levels of physical activity, which has created an unhealthy population where diet pills, processed foods, and prescription medications are staples.

Defining Health and Disease

What is health, anyway? The definition of *health*,[5] as well as the definition of *disease*,[6] is important to establish from the start. *Health* is certainly not merely "the state of the organism when it functions without evidence of disease or abnormality," as stated by *Stedman's Medical Dictionary*.[7] *Disease*, according to *Doorland's Medical Dictionary*, is "a definite pathological process having a characteristic set of signs and symptoms. It may affect the whole body or any of its parts, and its etiology, pathology, and prognosis may be known or unknown."[8] Sounds pretty bad, whatever it is, like a top-secret CIA agent gone AWOL, as in Bourne, Jason Bourne.

In any case, I believe *health* has been defined for far too long as the absence of disease. I define *health* in terms of *thriving, not just surviving*, optimizing and maximizing our potential for healthy living, not dealing with health issues when we can no longer ignore them. Ask yourself, is it reasonable to suppose that the treatment of disease may be off the mark if the definition we use to define the desired state of being is cast in negative terms? Treatment focus should be placed instead on the positive state of well-being, with efforts to support and strengthen the body's systems that allow us to function optimally. When that is not achievable, we should strive hard to identify and address the dysfunction(s) that are the root cause of a particular disease, even after years of dysfunction. Surely there is a time and a place in the practice of medicine to suppress symptoms, especially in emergency medical intervention, but this is clearly a temporary solution to save life, not a remedy or normative approach for long-term, sustainable health, healing, and vitality.

Evaluating various ways of defining health and considering the biomedical model of medicine in light of Christian theology, Baylor philosophy professors James A. Marcum and Robert B. Kruschwitz offered this conclusion:

> If a patient were merely a body-machine that is reducible to various separate body parts, then

health would simply be the absence of disease or of any malfunctioning part that hinders the efficient running of the body. . . . It is not surprising that there is a crisis in modern medicine, given its reductive understanding of health. Patients are not body-machines, but persons with concerns about their physical, mental, and spiritual being-in-the-world. Any adequate notion of health must include an account of well-being and wholeness which takes into consideration these concerns and fears.[9]

It is one thing to say what health is not, and as I have suggested it is quite another to say what health is. Many physicians and healthcare workers find the question "How do you define health?" a good question, as though this was never addressed in their four-plus years of medical school or, if it was, is not something they think about every day. One of my goals is to encourage all of us to think long and hard about the multitude of connections between health, healing, and faith as we consider our healthcare system and all the talk about reforming it. We must deal with moral weakness, first in our own lives and in the church, and then in society and its structures as well. Professor and author Abigail Rian Evans, in her book *Redeeming Marketplace Medicine*, proposes a challenging set of guidelines for the ongoing discussion about defining health, which Christians must do as biblically as possible:

The unique aspects of the biblical definition of health are as follows: (1) it is based on a doctrine of humankind as a unity—both within us and with our environment and community; (2) its definition[s] of health as wholeness and of sickness as brokenness include a spiritual dimension; (3) it orients us to health instead of sickness; (4) its primary goal is others' health, not our own; (5) it broadens healing to include any activity that moves us toward wholeness; and (6) it understands healers as persons who move us toward healing. These aspects provide the foundation for a radically different understanding of health care.[10]

Health Gives Freedom to Live and Love

Incorrectly defining health is a problem that goes far beyond our healthcare system because, from God's vantage point, we are His holy sanctuaries. We are His vessels. Many Christians disregard the fact that their bodies are God's holy dwelling place and that our Westernized lifestyles are destroying His temple. Thus, Christians are not able to live out their lives optimally, according to God's purpose, while plagued with fatigue or depression or falling ill to chronic lifestyle diseases. The simple fact is that illness is a form of bondage because it limits one's freedom and potential. Listen to a number of Scripture passages that establish what should be normal:

- Psalm 119:4: "I will walk about in freedom, for I have sought out your precepts."
- 2 Corinthians 3:17: "Now the Lord is the Spirit, and where the Spirit of the Lord is, there is freedom."
- Galatians 5:1: "It is for freedom that Christ has set us free. Stand firm, then, and do not let yourselves be burdened again by a yoke of slavery."

- John 8:36: "So if the Son sets you free, you will be free indeed."

Thus the Bible teaches that God wants His children to enjoy lives of freedom as we live in accordance with the greatest purpose for which He has created us—to love as Christ loves (John 13:34–35; Luke 10:27).

This Is Not Your Typical Health Book

This is not your typical health book encouraging you to *eat this, not that, or to do this, not that*. The reality is that almost everyone understands the difference between a good thought and a bad thought, healthy food and junk food (fruit versus candy), and the benefits of being physically active versus a sedentary lifestyle. Many people have at least some knowledge, but they often lack the courage, in today's culture, to admit the discrepancy between what we know and how we live. Therefore, the question for most of us is not what to do but *why* we continue to make the wrong choices when we know our choices are not good for us. It's not that we don't believe that eating healthfully or being active is better for us. But in any given moment only one belief wins out to the point of dictating our actions. Many times it's our unconscious, deceptive beliefs—beliefs such as "I have no time," "I need that drink of alcohol to relax," "This extra scoop of ice cream will make me feel better," and the like—that ultimately win out. Very often, these subtle lies become the principles that dictate our actions and work against what we know would be better for us. So how do we combat lies? With the truth— "the truth will set you free" (John 8:23). As Christians we say we value God's Word, but do we really? I believe that there is a large disconnect with Christians in our country between what we do and what we say we value, because what we value is evident by our actions, not merely what we say. God has a lot to say about health, but our actions as the body of Christ display that we do not truly value health—meaning that we do not truly value *all* of God's Word.

This book is designed to help us become grounded in His truth with regard to caring for our bodies—His temples, His vessels. In the beginning, we will discuss the truth clearly taught in Scripture that we reflect God's divine nature in that we are created in His image and likeness, and that in response we should stand in awe and wonder of Him and His amazing creation, the human body (chap.1).

Next, we will explore the purpose and meaning of the ancient tabernacle and temple and how they parallel the new covenant temple, which is literally our body, not only our individual body but also the role we have as a member of the body of the Christ, the church. We should stand in wonder that we have become a new creation in Christ Jesus with the Holy Spirit living in us (chap. 2).

We will also discuss that in this day and age caring for His temple must become even more intentional, since the modern conveniences of technology and processed foods that affect our lifestyles make it so easy and convenient to destroy God's temple (chap. 3).

With this knowledge, we will have a better understanding of why we need to move beyond motivation toward inspiration to better care for God's dwelling place as we serve His purpose for our lives. We will explore the truth that what we do affects not only our own generation but also the ones to come (chap. 4). You see, God has given us through His Word the ability to establish and discern healthy boundaries that will allow us to have and enjoy life to its fullest (chap. 5).

Additionally, this book will reveal the truths about the mind-body relationship with regard to health. It will focus on a connection between Scripture and science that will show how our bodies are impacted by our thoughts, prayers, and the desires of our heart (chap. 6).

In reading this book you may uncover some revelations with regard to strongholds (areas of your life that are occupied by something other than God) of which you may not previously have been aware. We will examine the biblical concept that although "all things" are now permissible, not all things are beneficial or constructive (1 Cor. 6:12; 10:23). This principle relates to the physiology of comfort food (junk food); the detrimental effects, both physical and spiritual, of using food for comfort; and our need to turn to God for comfort in our times of struggle and hardship (chap. 7).

Finally, we will discover the benefits of physical movement, as well as explore the concept of "moving" upon God's Word (putting into practice God's Word, whether something you hear individually from Him or something you read in Scripture). We will discuss how both aspects of "movement" will provide a positive stimulus for our minds and for strengthening our faith. We will learn that we need to move into an educated state of awareness because we live in a fast-paced world where we aren't fully aware of who we are and how what we do affects not only ourselves but also those around us (chap. 8).

We are to live faithfully in this time and culture where God has placed us. However, many are trying to find a healthy balance between unhealthy extremes. This book is not intended to provide a road map to that healthy balance; bear in mind that a healthy, balanced life does not mean "a balanced life with a little bit of God added in." Health is achieved when all the systems of our body are balanced and working together in proper function. When we take this seriously, in terms both of honoring God's Word and of honoring His dwelling place—His vessel, His temple—we will have a balanced life and overall good health (chap. 9).

As we move forward, my prayer is that our hearts may be softened, that we may be aware of the destructive strongholds in our lives, and that we will experience more of the Holy Spirit. I pray that as we approach a fully aligned life that brings us the health we need and desire, we will be better able to serve our Father in heaven. God has called us to more than we could ever imagine, and through His presence and strength I pray that we develop into healthier people, better equipped to do His will.

CHAPTER 1

We Are a Creation

"A simple man believes anything, but a prudent man gives thought to his steps."

Proverbs 14:15

"Let us have faith that right makes might, and in that faith, let us, to the end, dare to do our duty as we understand it."

Abraham Lincoln, "Cooper Union Address," February 27, 1860

Have you ever asked yourself, "Who am I?" "Why am I here?" "How did I get here?" Or the really serious one . . . "What difference do I make?" While many of us have pondered these questions, oftentimes it is easy to become overwhelmed by the vastness and the seeming intangibility of the answers we seek. Therefore, we end up spending many of our days just going through the motions—purposeless.

If you'll allow me to walk with you through a process (this process might possibly stretch your brain but stick with it), I would love to show you throughout the course of this book that there are answers to these questions. Each of us has been created, not only on purpose but also for a purpose. We have a good and faithful Creator who has provided us with the information and knowledge we need to go beyond surviving through a life of just going through the motions. My prayer is that the answers to these questions will inspire each of us to intentionally live healthier and thriving lives, dedicated to the glory of God. What would be the point of caring for ourselves if we were not created for a purpose. Sadly, this is precisely the dead-end sticking point where many people, young and old, find themselves. They have been sold a bill of goods and have bought in to lies and misinformation about who and what they are from God's perspective.

What we do, how we think, and how we care for ourselves do matter, and each of our lives has a higher purpose. The Bible is the greatest written source of purpose for human life, and in Acts 13:36 Paul says, "For when David had served God's purpose in his own generation, he fell asleep." We're all going to die someday. But by the end of our days, will we have served God's purpose in our generation? Instead of merely going through the motions, we can be living more fulfilled lives by realizing that each of us has been fashioned by the Creator as a vessel to effectively serve *His* purpose.

This book is meant to take us on a journey. It is important to do some soul searching to discover our true state of mind with regard to what we believe, because our beliefs ultimately determine our actions. If we choose to be left in the dark concerning our underlying beliefs, our state of mind, or the potentially destructive food choices we make, we will falter in any quest to reach God's intended design and purpose for our lives, both spiritually and physically. I'm talking about minimizing dysfunction and maximizing proper function in all aspects of life—that each of us get into a right relationship with God and get our bodies working the way God created them to work.

This book is directly focused on shedding light on these subjects. I will point out that by design, there are practical and biblical guidelines for us to live healthy, fulfilling, and thriving lives. Some of this is common sense, and some of it is revealed in God's Word, the Bible. As contradictory as many people would have you think this is, the universal truths in this book are concisely aligned with biblical truths, while at the same time, to the best of today's technological ability, scientifically based and proven. God is not opposed to science. As a matter of fact, He engineered the universe in such a way that more and more scientific truth waits for the curious human mind to uncover it. The use of science in this book is not intended to provide a foundation for truth or some kind of justification for our faith. Science is not perfect—remember, according to science, the world used to be flat! This previously believed fact shows us that as we advance in scientific discovery, previously "known" scientific truths are debunked and become irrelevant. The notion of a "flat" world is one example.

Rarely, however, will you hear the words "we were wrong" coming from the scientific community or in research articles where an author must backpedal in light of new research. We're all proud people who don't want to admit when we're wrong. But without this kind of trial and error, how can we hope to succeed in the future? Think how many failed tries it took Thomas Edison to discover the right material to use for the filament of his light bulb or how many failed political campaigns Abraham Lincoln had to endure before finally being elected!

Please don't misunderstand what I am saying; science has proved many theories, establishing them as laws of truth. For example, gravity: "what goes up must come down." However, as we've said scientific inquiry doesn't always or necessarily yield truth, Therefore, it is important that we start off rooted in universal truths. The Bible is the truth that has transcended history and is relevant to every culture and time. So, as we move forward, please remember that I have made every effort to ensure that the foundation of truth and knowledge provided in this book is biblically based. The best of what science has to offer is provided alongside, but only as an adjunct, to strengthen the arguments for the skeptics of the biblical truths presented in this book and to attempt to bridge any gaps that may occur in our earthy minds as to the relevance of Scripture in today's society. As the prophet Hosea lamented, "My people are destroyed from lack of knowledge" (Hosea 4:6). Knowledge is a foundational pillar for a purposeful life. When knowledge is *applied*, it becomes wisdom.

Starting Where Life and Death Began

Let's begin to answer the question "How did we get here?" The Bible begins answering this question with a sweeping description of how the earth was formed, how we are here—God created human beings in His image and likeness, using already created material from the earth (dust) that He animated with something immaterial from Himself (the breath of life)—and thus where we came from. God's story starts in the book of Genesis and explains our creation in these words: "Then the LORD God formed a man from the dust of the ground and breathed into his nostrils the breath of life, and the man became a living being" (Gen. 2:7). Thus, a human person is a unity of earthly stuff and spirit stuff, dirt and air, dust and a breath of divinity. So if somebody calls you a dirt bag, no worries—that's only half true!

Clay

Now after the world was made in all the splendor and glory of nature, something really bad happened. The first man, Adam, rebelled against his Creator and thus sinned—yes, with some help from the first woman, his wife, whom we know as Eve. This ethical lapse caused the entire human race to take quite a tumble that has since been called "the fall." With sin came death, as God had warned (Gen. 2:17; cf. Rom. 5:12). But through his gift of "common grace" God prevented humanity's immediate plunge into eternal death (separation from God forever) in order to restrain evil and wickedness and make possible the continuation of human life on earth, albeit in a fallen state. God explained to Adam the consequences of his sin and told him what would eventually happen to him, an embodied creature: "By the sweat of your brow you will eat your food until you return to the ground, since from it you were taken; for dust you are and to dust you will return" (Gen. 3:19). Death is the unnatural separation of the unified human person, dividing the spirit from the body. We weren't meant to live as disembodied spirits; in fact, that's what the resurrection of the dead is all about. But we'll get to that later . . .

Due to the simplicity of God's description in Genesis of the humble origin of the world and of the human race, it has been difficult for people, including learned scientists, to accept that these verses of ancient Scripture could be accurate and true. Could dust alone actually be responsible for constructing the complex elements and molecules that make up the human body? Over time, scientists have made great advancements, allowing us to identify and examine the components of a human being. In a 1982 *Readers Digest* article titled "*How Life on Earth Began,*" our humble beginning is described in the simplest of terms: "The Bible says that God scooped up a handful of *clay* and breathed life into it."

Curiously, at that time researchers at NASA's Ames Research Center concluded that metal-bearing clays probably played a pivotal part in joining together the basic building blocks of life. "I have a feeling," said Dr. James Lawless, one of the experimenters, "that the first living organisms might have been about half-*clay*."[11] Now fast forward to 2004, where researchers writing in the *International Journal of Astrobiology* said, "We have recently described a laboratory demonstration of the replication of membrane vesicles."[12]

Translation: there have to be cell membranes composed of fatty acids for our life to occur. Without them, our cells could not function. Later in the article the researchers added how this may have occurred: "We were able to show that RNA bound to the surface of particles of the *clay* mineral montmorillonite could become encapsulated within fatty acid vesicles assembled by the *clay*."[13] I show you this research because it demonstrates that *clay* contains the proper components for our cellular membrane to be formed, thus allowing life to occur, because we need cell membranes to sustain our life.

Up to this day and time science has not been able to provide answers to the question "How did we get here?" As you can see, science is slowly catching up to understanding God's work of creation and His truth written about it in the book of Genesis. The Christian scientist has an advantage when it comes to interpreting the reality of nature: "In your [God's] light we see light" (Ps. 39:9). Whatever the connection is between clay and the essential building blocks of life, trying to figure it out through scientific research alone, without using Scripture to assist the light of reason, sets up a perpetual "so close and yet so far" sort of situation. As journalist Amanda Bower points out in an article on neurobiology, "The great irony of human intelligence is that the only species on Earth capable of reason, complex-problem solving, long-term planning and consciousness understands so little about the organ that makes it all possible—the brain."[14] Human beings and the so-called natural world share much the same irony. Unless we approach science and Scripture, as well as reason and faith, on terms appropriate to each; bathe ourselves in humility; and pray for wisdom from God to help us understand how all of these things go together, we will always remain "so close and yet so far" from the truth.

Water

To solidify this answer to the proverbial question "Where did we come from?" I want to give you some additional facts. The human body, on average, is made up of approximately 70 percent water (the same percentage as the earth). I think this is an interesting parallel for two reasons.

First, we started to look for life on Mars when we identified its polar icecap, evidence that water may have been flowing on that planet at some point in time. Why is this interesting? Because it points to the scientific fact that a search for life is a search for water. Without water we cannot live.

The second reason I find this interesting is that Jesus is described in the Bible as the One who gives "living water" that brings life to the soul (John 4:10, 13–14). Water was not as convenient to obtain or keep in the time of Jesus as it is today with indoor plumbing, yet water was as much a necessity for life then as it is today. Just as the physical body needs water to continue living, so does the human spirit. Jesus gives us the "essential fluid" that satisfies the true spiritual needs of every human being. The apostle John later explains that this "living water," flowing like a river out of a believing person's heart, refers to God's Spirit (John 7:37–39). God earlier in the Scriptures refers to Himself as "the fountain of living water" (Jer. 2:13; 17:13). Water equals life. Without God the soul, due to the effects of sin, will eventually die. A soul is another way of referring to a living being, person, or creature. The human soul is thirsty, and we try to quench that thirst with many things of the world that only temporarily satisfy us, but eventually we are thirsty again. The only thing that can truly quench the thirst of a human spirit is being satisfied by the Giver of living water, Jesus Christ. The psalmist anticipated this truth in saying, "With you is the fountain of life" (Ps. 36:9). Can you see the connection?

God created the earth, and God created the human body, making both approximately 70 percent water so life could come to light. God also provides the living water (the Spirit of Christ) that sustains and feeds our soul and gives life to our mortal bodies (Rom. 8:11). Without this living water, our spirit and soul will eventually die, just as our physical body eventually dies if we do not drink any water. Good ole H_2O is some pretty important stuff on more than one level.

What's So Special about the Number *Three*?

Let me provide one more example of God's divine order with regard to the question How did we get here? This example has to do with numbers, but first let me explain something. When I meet with a patient for the first time, I gather as much information about the patient's body as I can: such as symptoms, physical signs, lab work, X-rays, and the like. Initially, all this information appears to be chaotic, but when I evaluate the data patterns start to emerge as I contrast the information against the proper or optimal design and function of the human body. Thus my brain is always looking for patterns congruent with design. What I am about to share with you in answer to this question of the origin of life is not intended to be a bunch of theological or philosophical proofs, but simply some observations I have made that clarify to me that the creation is intentional and orderly in its design. This example is found in the patterns I see of the number *three* in God's Word and in human life and experience. We begin with creation before making some observations about life and finally returning to Scripture.

In the Creation Account

From the beginning of creation the number *three* has had a special significance. On the first day God said "Let there be light" (Gen. 1:3), after which He separated it from darkness. On the second day God said, "Let there be an expanse between the waters to separate water from water" (Gen. 1:6). God called the expanse "sky," thus allowing us to have air to breathe to make life for us possible. On the third day God said, "Let the water under the sky gather into one place, and let dry ground appear" (Gen. 1:9).

It was on this third day that the earth was separated from the water in preparation for land life. This allowed for vegetation to grow, as fruit-bearing plants and trees all had seeds allowing for growth and reproduction. It was at this moment in time, on the third day, that the earth was physically and chemically complete, ready to sustain plant life—the same plant life God said would be ours for food (Gen. 1:29). The first three days marked the completion of forming (heavens; sky and sea, and land) what God would then fill on the final three days (sun, moon, and stars; birds and fish; and land animals and man).

In Human Life and Experience

So in the Bible's creation story the number *three* appears to be symbolic of completeness or entirety. In human life, our physical body goes through three stages or phases: conception and birth, life, and death. Our time here on earth, too, is divided into three stages: the past, the present, and the future. Theologians, philosophers, and psychologists can debate till the kingdom comes whether the human being is a dichotomy (body and soul/spirit) or a trichotomy (body, soul, and spirit)—not to be confused with a tracheotomy! Alluding to this number in another way, our bodies can be recognized as consisting of three component parts: physical, chemical, and emotional. Using still another paradigm, we might also suggest that our being is made up of the mind, the body, and the spirit.

Now, as I've mentioned above, here are three separate and distinct aspects of human life—our time here on earth, our physical body, and the essence of our being. Where does one end and another take up? Is there a time or part of life where these three aspects cease to overlap and interact with each other? The answer is that they do not begin and end as separate aspects, because they are mutually dependent on each other. Let me offer a picture to which most of us can relate to illustrate the integration and interconnection within the unity of body and soul in the human person.

Imagine speeding down the highway and seeing a police officer with his radar gun pointed right at you. The police officer looks you in the eye—you know you are in trouble, your heart starts to pound, and your leg muscles tighten up. What has just happened? Your emotional reaction was triggered by the fear of getting caught and getting a speeding ticket, which released certain chemicals (adrenaline), which changed the physical function of your body by increasing your heart rate and causing your muscles to tense up.

You see, the physical, chemical, and emotional aspects of the body are all connected. You cannot separate the emotions from the chemicals and not affect the physical body. That's why the proper view of a human being is to see a person as a whole, not a collection of disconnected parts. Disconnection brings dysfunction, disease, disability, and ultimately death. We were made to be whole, healthy, and at peace with God and nature. We are to be walking with Him in the world He created to be our home and our place for fellowship with Him. The Hebrew word *shalom* expresses all of this at once: "The general meaning behind the root *š-l-m* is of completion and fulfillment—of entering into a state of wholeness and unity, a restored relationship." Related terms are "peace, prosperity, well, health, completeness, safety."[15] Scores of people, as well as the world itself, could use a lot more of God's shalom, and this can only be achieved if we first realize that everything about our existence is connected.

In the Bible

The significance of the number *three* is found throughout the Bible. For instance, there are many divine attributes or descriptors of who God is and what He is like, some of which we share with God (e.g., wisdom, power, holiness, justice, goodness, and truth) and others of which are true only of Him (e.g., infinity, eternality, and immutability). I've noticed three of God's attributes that stand out by their prefix: *omni*potence (all-powerful), *omni*science (all-knowing or all-wise), and *omni*presence (everywhere present). It's pretty amazing to realize, as pastor, author, and blogger Tim Challies points out, that "God is not simply the sum of his attributes. His attributes are not separate from one another, but each one modifies or qualifies the others."[16]

The number *three* also relates to what is perhaps the greatest display of God's power—the gospel itself, the "power of God for the salvation of everyone who believes" (Rom. 1:16–17). The gospel message is "that Christ died for our sins according to the Scriptures, that he was buried, that he was raised on the *third day* according to the Scriptures," after which Jesus appeared to his disciples and to hundreds of others (1 Cor. 15:1–7, esp. v. 4). It occurs to me that there may be some connection between the *third day* of creation and the *third day* of the new creation. Whatever the case, Jesus' resurrection ended the old order of things and inaugurated a new order to life, so that calling it "new creation" is no exaggeration:[17] "Our Savior, Christ Jesus . . . has destroyed death and has brought life and immortality to light through the gospel" (1 Tim. 1:10). Someday He's going to wipe away the tears from our eyes; "there will be no more death or mourning or crying or pain, for the old order of things has passed away" (Rev. 21:4). A little theology, a little math, a little speeding ticket—it all connects, just as the body and soul are connected.

The number *three* also comes into play with regard to the Israelite place of worship within the temple, as described in the Old Testament. The Most Holy Place was a cube of twenty cubits (1 Kings 6:20), each consisting of three parts: the court, the Holy Place, and the sanctuary. However, the best biblical example of completeness is the Trinity—one God in three persons, or one *What* and three *Whos*. The three entities or persons—God the Father, Jesus Christ the Son, and the Holy Spirit—are all one in nature or essence, yet the functions of the Father, the Son, and the Spirit are different. Thus the one God exists in a triunity of interrelationships, a holy and perfect "community" of three.

Marriage (two persons yet one flesh), the church (many members yet one body), and our society (many citizens yet one nation) all depend on and can reflect this unity within diversity idea that comes from the mysterious and simultaneous oneness and threeness of God. Biblical scholar and theologian E. W. Bullinger suggested that "the number *three* points us to what is real, essential, perfect, substantial, complete, and divine."[18] The consistent reappearance of this number with relation to human life provides additional evidence in my mind that we are in fact of divine origin.

Thinkers or Believers or Both?

I find it interesting that many people ask me how I can be a researcher and science-minded educator and physician, yet still believe in the creation "fairy tale," as opposed to the science of evolution. Let me be clear: I do believe that evolutionary adaptations occur on a micro level. For example, the obesity epidemic, which you will soon learn about, is largely an effect of environmental issues stemming from changes brought about by the Industrial Revolution—changes such as processed food, sedentary lifestyles, and pollution. I believe that everything was created from something. I also believe that a higher power is responsible for the intricate design of all creation.

However, the way the scientific evolution theory (note that I said *theory*, not scientific law, principle, or dogma) is taught, it is a large stretch for my mind to think that no one initiated the process of origins by creating something from nothing! I am not going to delve into details about various misleading notions of evolutionary theory that are being taught today in secular educational establishments as accepted truth and scientific law. But the book *I Don't Have Enough Faith to Be an Atheist* by Norman L. Geisler and David Limbaugh does a very good job of examining these notions in detail.[19]

Charles Darwin, the father of the theory of evolution, in a letter to the skeptic John Fordyce, wrote, "In my most extreme fluctuations I have never been an atheist in the sense of denying the existence of a God."[20] From my scientific perspective, God either exists or He doesn't exist. It's not possible for Him to exist for me and not for you. It would be like me saying that water exists because I believe in water. How absurd for someone else to choose not to believe in water and to declare that, therefore, it does not exist for them. Human beings, whether scientists or theologians or laypersons, can neither prove nor disprove God's existence. Even the Bible doesn't try to do so; from verse one it simply assumes that God is: "In the beginning God . . ." Those opening words mark the point of departure for every theory that claims otherwise.

As for me, I believe God exists. And I see it as a much more difficult choice *not* to believe in God. Atheists ("there is no God") and agnostics ("I don't or can't know if there is a God") have a much harder task, in terms of supporting their stance, than I do. British novelist and scholar C. S. Lewis exposed why disbelieving is so difficult: "I believe in Christianity as I believe that the sun has risen. Not only because I see it, but because by it I see everything else."[21] Elsewhere, in commenting on the influence certain Christian thinkers—such as the Scottish author and poet George MacDonald and the English writer G. K. Chesterton—had on him, Lewis said, "A young man who wishes to remain a sound Atheist cannot be too careful of his reading. There are traps everywhere—'Bibles laid open, millions of surprises,' as Herbert says, 'fine nets and stratagems.' God is, if I may say it, very unscrupulous."[22]

Whether you are a believer who needs to think or a thinker who needs to believe, eventually every one of us must deal with a fundamental limitation—our inability to figure it all out *without God*. "And *without faith* it is impossible to please God" (Heb. 11:6, emphasis added). Scottish Christian minister and teacher Oswald Chambers penetrates to the heart of the matter with his usual incisiveness: "The real attitude of sin in the heart towards God is that of being without God; it is pride, the worship of myself, that is the great atheistic fact in human life."[23] Christian apologist and author Ravi Zacharias puts it bluntly: "God has put enough into the world to make faith in Him a most reasonable thing, and He has left enough out to make it impossible to live by sheer reason or observation alone."[24]

The Miracle of Life

After examining the truth according to the Scriptures and such facts about our existence in its simplest form, it only makes sense that somebody created something out of nothing. So my question then becomes how one can choose not to believe in the Creator and in nature as God's creation. In fact, let's look at the miracle of life in terms of the human anatomy (an area of study that I especially enjoy) to better understand how wonderfully our body is made.

The psalmist David enthused in praise to God, "For you created my innermost being, you knit me together in my mother's womb. I praise you because I am fearfully and wonderfully made. Your works are wonderful and I know that full well" (Ps. 139:13–14).

The human body is the most amazing phenomenon I have ever come across. Let's talk about just one particularly fascinating aspect of the human body. When we were inside our mother's womb filled with amniotic fluid, we didn't breathe for two reasons: initially our lungs were not developed, and once they were sufficiently developed for life outside the womb we would have drowned had we exercised our breathing ability.

To prevent this, according to design, blood is first oxygenated in the mother's lungs and then oxygen is transferred by blood to the developing baby via the umbilical cord. Since the baby's lungs are not working while in the womb, the little one has a hole in the heart called the foramen ovale ("oval window"). It allows blood to flow right over to the other chamber, so the heart can pump and circulate the blood throughout the body of the baby without passing through the lungs. Amazingly, when a baby takes its first breath the foramen ovale shuts (except in rare cases) and the blood instantaneously travels to the lungs to be oxygenated. How marvelous is that? How can you not believe in God when His creation is so absolutely miraculous?

The likelihood that we came from single-cell organisms, over time became apes, and from apes morphed into the amazing human beings we are today is in my opinion literally ridiculous. As English astronomer and mathematician Fred

Hoyle, who coined the term "big bang," famously stated in *Nature* magazine, "The chance that higher life forms might have emerged by chance is comparable with the chance that a tornado sweeping through a junkyard might assemble a Boeing 747 from the materials therein."[25]

When people ask me why I believe in creation, I reply with the question "How can you *not*?" If someone examines closely the complexities of life, they will likely appreciate that the human body is an absolute marvel made with masterful, divine order. It amazes me that the second we take that first breathe—*bam!*—the previously essential hole in our heart closes and our lungs activate.

Let's examine the fact that we do indeed start our lives before birth through the union of a component coming from the mother (the egg) and a component from the father (the sperm). Everything about the amazing human body starts when they unite! When I was in undergraduate school, one of the most phenomenal classes I took was developmental biology. In this class my professor had us do an experiment allowing us to observe under the microscope conception taking place between sea urchin eggs and sperm.[26] Before we started the experiment, he said something very interesting: "Pay close attention, because when the sperm penetrates the egg and becomes one, you will see a flash of light." During that experiment the flash of light occurred, just as my professor had said.

In my then youthful age and spiritually unsaved state, I was not able to realize the significance of what had just occurred. However, I knew that life is dependent upon energy and that a lack of energy by definition is death. Light is a form of energy, and when I saw that flash of light, I knew I had just witnessed the formation of life. What I did not know then but have since learned is that Jesus is called "the true Light, which lighteth every man that cometh into the world" (John 1:9 KJV), thus making the fertilized human egg (zygote) at that very second of conception "a living being." With this knowledge at hand, I have to ask, Who is man to determine when a zygote or embryo should be considered a living being? If you were to witness what I witnessed that day, I would dare assume that you, like me, would unequivocally know that life begins at the moment of conception. How can anyone, I ask myself, *not* believe in creation? I have enough evidence that I can believe it beyond a reasonable doubt. Can you?

Based on the landscape of knowledge that we have just covered, I hope you realize that we are here through God's divine power to serve His purpose. We have focused indirectly on the questions of who we are, why we are here, and what difference we make here, but we're going to keep at it in what follows. I believe it is our responsibility to treat life with respect and reverence because we are not our own. We are a creation of God, a creation that, because of our sin, He redeemed (bought back) at a dear price—by sacrificing His only Son in our place so we might one day have eternal life with Him (Gen. 1:26–27; 1 Cor. 6:20; John 3:16). For this we should be profoundly and forever thankful. Are your actions reflecting your gratitude?

CHAPTER 2

God's Purpose for Our Bodies

*"If God only used perfect people, nothing would get
done. God will use anybody if you are available."*
Rick Warren

*"For we are God's workmanship, created in Christ Jesus
to do good works, which God prepared
in advance for us to do."*
Ephesians 2:10

N ow that we share an understanding of God's creation, brought into being through His omnipotent strength, we will shift gears to better understand how we should view His creation. The Bible teaches that our physical bodies are the dwelling place of the Holy Spirit: "Do you not know that your bodies are temples of the Holy Spirit, who is in you, whom you have received from God? You are not your own" (1 Cor. 6:19). Imagine that! *Our body is God's temple*, and He dwells among us. If for no other reason than that, we should take care of our bodies in order that we may glorify Him in all our actions!

The temple in which God dwelt during the Old Testament period is different from that in which He dwells after the promised deliverer Jesus Christ went to die on the cross to take away the sin of the world. In our Western society, the concept of a "temple" is pretty far removed from most people's train of thought. We tend to think of a temple in terms of some archaic religion or of broken-down ruins straight out of a scene from Indiana Jones. Before we can move forward and appreciate the idea and reality that *we* are God's dwelling place, we need to go back in time to get some background, since the analogy of the human body as a temple is perhaps a difficult concept to grasp if one does not know the history and beauty behind it. Stick with me here as it's important that we review the historical background of God's dwellings and places for us to worship; this will allow us to identify similarities between the Old Testament and New Testament temples that are important for us to relate to in terms of the temple that is our body as we live in our modern-day society.

How the Idea of a Temple Developed

The idea of a temple goes way back to ancient times. According to archaeologists, Göbekli Tepe, located in southeastern Turkey, "has been interpreted as the oldest humanmade place of worship yet discovered."[27] Its first structures are thought to have been built, perhaps by hunter-gatherers, as early as 10,000 B.C.,[28] at least according to an evolutionary view of the world and human history. The evidence at the site (identifiable animal bones, along with sculptures and relics) suggests to Klaus Schmidt of the German

Archaeological Institute that "the people who created these massive and enigmatic structures came from great distances," including pilgrimages to make animal sacrifices.[29]

All of this is very interesting, yet who really knows about the dates when you get that far back in time.[30] What we do know from Scripture, and from Genesis 1–11 in particular, is that these human beings were created by God in His image and likeness (Gen. 1:27; 5:1–3ff.), and we can conclude that they built this temple sometime after God expelled Adam and Eve from the Garden of Eden (Gen. 3:22–24). We'll get to the story of Cain and Abel in connection with the activity of worship as a forerunner leading up to the construction of altars, temples, and cities built in this period. But one verse at the end of the Cain and Abel story mentions another brother, named Seth, followed by these words: "At that time men began to call on the name of the LORD" (Gen. 4:26). What a curious statement of historical development, loaded with implications, from which we can attempt to draw good and necessary assumptions. Calling on the name of the Lord certainly has something to do with the worship of God, and what the excavations of ancient ruins make clear is that altars and temples became an important part of humanity's search for God.

Why Temples Were Built

What is so significant about the fact that people from ancient times built altars and temples? And why did they do it? After all, constructing a temple required a lot of effort, especially without modern construction equipment. Experts of the Göbekli Tepe site estimate that "at least 500 people were required to hew the 10- to 50-ton stone pillars from local quarries, move them from as far as a quarter-mile away, and erect them."[31] And yet the surviving ziggurats of Mesopotamia (Sumerian, Akkadian, Assyrian, and Babylonian); the pyramids of Egypt; Greco-Roman temples; and temples from the vast Eastern cultures, such as the largest Hindu temple complex in the world, Angkor Wat in Siem Reap, Cambodia,[32] still stand to this day in silent testimony to the beliefs that moved ancient peoples to such remarkable architectural feats, some of which remain a mystery to this day.

But why did the ancients do it? What inspired them, and to what end, to put forth such effort? To obtain blessing on their crops and herds? To appease the spirits of deceased ancestors and restore harmony within the tribe (or bring balance to the force, like Luke Skywalker)? To prepare for safe transport to the afterlife? Yes, probably all of the above and more, depending on which ancient culture and which ancient religious beliefs we're talking about. In describing the ancient worldview and cosmology inherited by the Sumerians—a worldview and cosmology that "would be received as truth by almost all societies that followed . . . right down to the threshold of modern times"—scholar and writer Thomas Cahill asks in his book *The Gifts of the Jews*,

> Why were all earthly temples and sacred places built
> at the highest point available to the builders? Because
> this is the place nearest the sky. And why is the most
> sacred space nearest the sky? Because the sky is the
> divine opposite of life on earth, home of all that is
> eternal in contrast to the moral life of earth. . . . The
> regions above man's reach, the starry places, are
> invested with the divine majesty of the transcendent,

of absolute reality, of everlastingness. Such places are the dwelling of the gods.[33]

The wisdom of God in the Scriptures reveals the human reach for the divine in these words: "[God] has also set eternity in the hearts of men; yet they cannot fathom what God has done from beginning to end. . . . God does it so that men will revere him" (Eccles. 3:11, 14). Thus, at the risk of overgeneralizing, temples were built by people from ancient times to this day in an attempt to reach beyond themselves to worship the divine, and one religious practice regularly associated with temple worship is animal sacrifice.[34]

Why Animals Were Sacrificed

Now why did people make animal sacrifices a part of their worship of deity? This was a pretty extreme measure to take, one that implied a great offense against God, necessitating that the blood of an innocent creature must be shed. While we can wonder about all the ways in which the world would have been different if Adam had chosen not to sin, one thing is for certain: blood sacrifices would never have been necessary in that paradise, because neither law nor forgiveness is needed when there is no sin (Rom. 5:13; Heb. 9:22). But the reality is that we live in a fallen world. The first animals to be sacrificed were those that the Lord God killed to make coverings of skin for Adam and Eve (Gen. 3:21). Then in Genesis 4 we read that the first children born were brothers: Cain, who became a farmer, and Abel, who became a shepherd.

As time went on Cain brought some fruits of the soil as an offering, while Abel brought fat portions for animal sacrifice, some of the firstborn of his flock. No explicit mention of altars or temples has yet been made; this is the first recorded instance in the Bible of worship of this kind. Unlike Cain, Abel and his offering received the Lord's favor. The offerings the brothers presented clearly differed in kind, but what evidently differed much more were the thoughts and intents of the hearts of those who presented them. Hebrews 11:3 comments, "By faith Abel offered God a better sacrifice than Cain did. By faith he was commended as a righteous man, when God spoke well of his offerings." Likewise, 1 John 1:12 leaves no doubt as to what was in Cain's heart: "Do not be like Cain, who belonged to the evil one and murdered his brother. And why did he murder him? Because his own actions were evil and his brother's were righteous."

Cain's ensuing rage put him in great danger! Despite God's offers of grace, inviting him to get a grip and do what was right so he also could be accepted, Cain instead allowed sin to get the best of him. He gave in to the wicked thoughts in his angry heart and committed the world's first cold-blooded murder. Cain's act spoke volumes about who he had become. Author and pastor Paul David Tripp sets this before us in no uncertain terms: "Human beings by their very nature are worshipers. Worship is not something we do; it defines who we are. You cannot divide human beings into those who worship and those who don't. Everybody worships; it's just a matter of what, or whom, we serve."[35] Who or what do you worship? Have you let certain things in your life slip into the place of God, thus edging him out of the center of your life? If so, keep reading. In the chapters to come some revelations may come to you!

"A City with a Tower That Reaches to the Heavens"

Cain went his way, while Seth, the son God sent Adam and Eve to replace Abel, fathered the line through whom God's promise of deliverance would be fulfilled. Few people walked with God in the generations before the flood; Enoch was a notable exception (Gen. 5:21–24). Humanity became so wicked, in fact, that God determined to destroy all life by a flood (Gen. 6:5–8). Following the story of Noah and the ark, by which God saved this righteous man and his family, Noah built an altar to the Lord and sacrificed burnt offerings on it (Gen. 8:20). Then we read about what might be considered the first temple mentioned in the Bible, which was perhaps also the world's first skyscraper, the Tower of Babel (Gen. 11:1–9).

Recall, in light of the expressed intent of these builders, Thomas Cahill's comments about building temples and other sacred places on the highest points: "Come, let us build ourselves a city, with a tower that reaches to the heavens, so that we may make a name for ourselves and not be scattered over the face of the whole earth" (Gen. 11:4). This project and its intent opposed God's purposes, and it was brought to a grinding halt when God by His common grace came down to see the tower and subsequently confused the common language everybody had to this point shared.

The entire enterprise devolved into a ridiculous and frustrating scene, as brick makers, bakers, and bricklayers were suddenly rendered incommunicado. But God's purpose toward humanity in all of this was ever gracious and ultimately redemptive (see Acts 2), aimed at restraining our human potential and capacity for even greater evil than that which had precipitated (no pun intended) the divine judgment and destruction of the world by the floodwaters (Genesis 6–7). Man's idea of and purpose for a city with a tower-temple wasn't what God had in mind, as the Lord later says through Isaiah the prophet: "As the heavens are higher than the earth, so are my ways higher than your ways and my thoughts than your thoughts" (Isa. 55:8–9).

Israel's Tabernacle in the Wilderness

Moving forward, the next time we read about a temple in relationship to God is when God gave Moses the tabernacle blueprint after the release of the Israelites from their four-hundred-year captivity in Egypt (Exod. 25:9; Heb. 8:5). Since God was now leading his people in their exodus from Egypt, in order for Him to dwell among them the construction of a movable tent-temple called the *tabernacle* was necessary. God said to Moses, "Have them make a sanctuary for me, and I will dwell among them" (Exod. 25:8). The Old Testament word for sanctuary is *miqdash*, a noun meaning a "holy or sacred place, a sanctuary."[36] This word designates that something has been sanctified or set apart as sacred or holy, as opposed to secular or common.

God wanted a place where He could dwell that was set apart from the rest of the world. In Exodus 26 we find the detailed instruction from God that was revealed to Moses at Mount Sinai, and to men and women in the land who were to make this portable sanctuary—the tabernacle. The cloth that formed the sides was woven as one would weave a fine evening gown, the wood for the frames was handled as though the end result would be fine furniture, and each section of the tabernacle was constructed with great care and exquisite attention to detail.[37]

Israel's Temple in Jerusalem

Eventually, when King Solomon constructed the first temple in ancient Jerusalem, he too followed instructions from the Lord. First Chronicles 6:32 tells us that the musicians "ministered with music at the tabernacle until Solomon built the temple of the LORD in Jerusalem. They carried out their work, following all the regulations handed down to them." Solomon is able to fulfill a lifelong dream of his father, David: "In the four hundred and eightieth year after the Israelites came out of Egypt, in the fourth year of Solomon's reign over Israel, in the month of Ziv, the second month, he began to build the temple of the LORD" (1 Kings 6:1). If we were to study the details of how this temple was to be built, we would find that God specified the use of the finest materials, such as pure gold; bronze; olive wood; cedar; and linens of blue, purple, and crimson (2 Chronicles 3; 1 Kings 6). No detail was ignored for the dwelling of the Lord, as the process and result created a sense of awe and wonder.[38] Eventually, however, what I like to call "Acquired Immunity to the Bright Shining Object Syndrome" kicked in. Let me describe what I mean.

Remember that Christmas morning when you, or perhaps your child, were in awe and wonder of their shiny new gift. At first it afforded so much joy and happiness, but eventually the newness wore off. Two weeks later the new toy had been cast aside, possibly never to be played with again.

Not every toy is lucky enough to be as loved as Woody or Buzz Lightyear!

Or how about when a newborn child enters the world? We all stare in wonder at the miracle of birth, and when the baby clinches our finger for the first time it brings tears to our eyes. However, we soon lose that sense of awe and wonder, especially as that child grows up and tests our boundaries.

The temple, initially a place of awe and wonder, was over the centuries to suffer misuse and abuse. Eventually it was plundered by the Babylonian king Nebuchadnezzar when his army breached the city walls of Jerusalem; it was subsequently burned, along with most of the city (2 Kings 25:8–21). Not surprisingly, *God did not take this desecration lightly.* In commenting on the undying significance of the Jerusalem temple and its destruction, professor and author Simon Goldhill points out:

> The Temple is never just a destroyed building. It has become the most potent symbol of the human search for a lost ideal, an image of former greatness and greatness to come. It is an idea that has prompted struggle, brutal war between cultures and nations, and some of the most moving poetry and art of the Western tradition. A history of the Temple can never be merely an architectural record, nor just an account of religious rituals. We need a special sort of archaeology for this great building of the world, archaeology that uncovers not so much rock and dust as the sedimented layers of human fantasy, politics and longing.[39]

The Babylonians worshiped many gods, and at one time Babylonia was the richest empire in the world. The city reflected that wealth in its extensive and highly decorated monuments, as well as in its indulgence in exotic goods from around the world. Prior to the destruction of the temple, Nebuchadnezzar had taken gold and silver vessels from it (2 Chron. 36:10). Years later Belshazzar, his son, threw a big feast and added injury to insult by using the silver and gold from the Jerusalem temple in a royal banquet (Dan. 5:1–3).

This empire consequently met the wrath of God and fell by divine judgment; Nebuchadnezzar's generational line perished for this misuse and destruction of God's temple and its holy articles. In Daniel 5 we read that a mysterious, disembodied "hand writing on the wall" spelled out "*Mene, Mene, Tekel, Parsin,*" meaning that God had numbered the days of the dynasty and was bringing it to an end. The Babylonians had been weighed on God's scales and found wanting, and their kingdom was to be divided and given to the Medes and Persians. That very night Belshazzar, the king of Babylonia, was slain and the kingdom was overtaken.

Jesus "Tabernacled" among Us

As you can see, God took great care in the construction of his earthly dwellings, the tabernacle and the temple, respectively. After these dwellings, God made his dwelling in a new temple, as "the Word [Jesus Christ] became flesh and made his dwelling among us" (John 1:14). What greater affirmation is there than the incarnation, the en-flesh-ment of the Son of God? Christian theology professor and author

Michael Wittmer draws out the rich implications of this truth about Jesus:

> The Word became flesh. Have you ever read the Christmas story as an affirmation of creation? That is precisely how John saw it. The Son of God not only created this physical world but also chose to become a part of it. God himself has acquired a human body. There is no stronger way to say that matter is good. How dare we suggest that the material world is somehow evil or beneath us? If matter is good enough for God, then whether we know it or not, it is plenty good for us.[40]

This adds meat, so to speak, to the meaning of the name *Immanuel*. Matthew 1:22–23 reports the messianic fulfillment of the prophecy in Isaiah 7:14: "All this took place to fulfill what the Lord had said through the prophet: 'The virgin will be with child and will give birth to a son, and they will call him Immanuel'—which means, 'God with us.'" The Lord God came and walked among us. There is no doubt that Jesus suffered misuse and abuse; He was ultimately nailed to the cross. But Jesus Himself, with reference to His body, had prophesied, "Destroy this temple, and I will raise it again in three days" (John 2:19).

Our Human Bodies, God's Dwelling Place

Now that we have covered the historical context of tabernacles, temples, and other places of worship, let's look at today's reality. When we accept Christ into our hearts, the Holy Spirit comes and dwells within us, and *we* become a new dwelling for Him. Why would God make us a new dwelling? There's much that we don't understand about God and His ways. He called all of creation "very good," though perhaps the reason He chooses to indwell us may be that, as copies of Himself, we are His most prized creations. Scripture records, "Then God said, Let us make mankind in our image, in our likeness, so that they may rule over the fish in the sea and the birds in the sky, over the livestock and all the wild animals, and over all the creatures that move along the ground. So God created mankind in his own image, in the image of God he created them; male and female he created them" (Gen. 1:26–27).

As far as we know from Scripture, only in humankind is there a dwelling place for God by His Spirit. God chooses to live in our hearts. Speaking to the church of Laodicea in John's vision, Jesus says, "Here I am. I stand at the door and knock. If anyone hears my voice and opens the door, I will come in and eat with him, and he with me" (Rev. 3:20). Jesus Christ actually lives within individual believers by the Holy Spirit, whom Paul, without batting an eyelash, calls "the Spirit," "the Spirit of Christ," and simply "Christ liv[ing] in you"—yes, Christ in us, the hope of glory (Rom 8:8–10; Col. 1:27).

Guess who inhabits the body of Christ and gives life to the people of God, both individually and collectively? Paul explains his theology of *the body* in the context of discussing the gifts of the Spirit God gives its members (redeemed people) who belong to Christ in order to build up the whole church: "The body is a unit, though it is made up of many parts; and though all its parts are many, they form one body. *So it is with Christ. For we were all baptized by one Spirit into one body*—whether Jews or Greeks, slave or free—and we were all given the one Spirit to drink" (1 Cor. 12:12–14, emphasis added).

God made humans in His likeness, as holy, set-apart beings! In 1 Peter 2:5 we read, "Present yourselves as building stones for the construction of a sanctuary vibrant with life, in which you'll serve as holy priests offering Christ-approved lives up to God" (The Message). Verse 9 says, "But you are the ones chosen by God, chosen for the high calling of priestly work, chosen to be a holy people, God's instruments to do His work and speak out for Him, to tell others of the night-and-day difference He made for you."

Are you a member of the body of Christ? God has been getting out the good news of His message that the Deliverer has come to clean up the mess we human beings have made of everything. The apostle Paul lived to preach this message. The weirder the setting and the more challenging the audience, the better he seemed to like it. Once in the ancient city of Athens he offered a fascinating explanation to a mixed audience (Jews and Gentiles) concerning God's involvement with and purpose for the destinies of the world's many nations, leading them finally to how all of this ties in to the gospel about Jesus Christ, whom God raised from the dead. But Paul also clarified something important about whether or not the one true God really spends time in ancient temples:

> The God who made the world and everything in it is *the Lord of heaven and earth and does not live in temples built by hands.* And he is not served by human hands, as if he needed anything, because he himself gives all men life and breath and everything

else. From one man he made every nation of men, that they should inhabit the whole earth; and he determined the times set for them and the exact places where they should live. *God did this so that men would seek him and perhaps reach out for him and find him*, though he is not far from each one of us. "For in him we live and move and have our being." As some of your own poets have said, "We are his offspring." (Acts 17:24–28, emphasis added)

Curious, isn't it, that human beings throughout the ages have built temples, including God's own people at His direction? Yet, as I've been saying, God's ultimate purpose went beyond being *with* His people to dwelling or living *within* us by His Spirit. God has gifted each one of us with (no, *as!*) a wonderful temple. As Paul puts it in 1 Corinthians 3:16, "Don't you know that you yourselves are God's temple and that God's Spirit lives in you?" What should we as human believers do with *or as* that temple? Just as honor was originally brought to the temple in Jerusalem, so honor should be brought to the God-made temple of our body. The temple of old was to be kept clean and in good repair; shouldn't we do the same with God's human temple? It took work to keep the manmade temple clean and in shape. This is true of our bodies, too. It takes work, but the end result is one of honor to the Creator. Work is a good thing (it may help us to recognize that work predates man's fall into sin). Work is something God does, and it's what we do when we care for, clean up, and repair our God-given temples. In so doing we bring Him honor and express our appreciation for what He has given us.

Moving beyond Motivation

In today's society we need to go beyond motivation in order to create permanent change in our lifestyle and habits as we honor God's temple. It is great to become motivated, but ultimately motivation dies out. Think of a car on a flat road. If you get behind the car and push it, you can use force to make it move and even gain some momentum. However, what happens if a slight hill impedes your progress? As the car meets more resistance, you must generate more force. Eventually, you will become fatigued from forcing the car to do something that the law of physics does not want to have happen. Motivation does the same thing for us; it forces us to do something against our presently held personal beliefs and inclinations. That's why motivation eventually dies.

New Year's Resolutions

Let's take a look at New Year's resolutions. The majority are related to the main topics of this book—better health and better life. In 2007 a research study was conducted involving more than 3,000 people who were attempting to achieve a range of resolutions, including losing weight, visiting the gym, quitting smoking, and drinking less alcohol. At the start of the study, 52 percent of the participants were confident of success. One year later only 12 percent had actually achieved their goal.[41]

How could it be that so few saw success? The answer is that when they began *they were motivated*. Motivation moves us to change our behavior to accomplish a goal. Thus, when we are motivated we are not only doing something that goes against our personal inclination, but we're typically doing it based on a selfish incentive—a WIIFM: What's in it for me? There is a basic fallacy in the notion that behavioral changes can be achieved for this reason.

As Christians, we especially need to understand that the things we do should not be about us, because *we're not our own*. I cannot project my values onto you; however, I believe that if through faith we have accepted Jesus Christ into our hearts and pledged our life's ultimate allegiance to Him alone, then we will strive to get our values in line with what God tells us in His Word He values. In order to facilitate a permanent change, we must be *inspired* by a power greater than ourselves.

If we do not think God cares about how we live, how we think, and what we eat, we are dead wrong; the enemy, Satan, has blinded us. There really is a devil, and he's not interested in your becoming a thriving vessel for God's use. No, he wants much less for you! (John 10:10). We need to become inspired, because *we are God's dwelling place*. We are His place, His tabernacle, the vehicles He uses to move about among us, *His vessel to share His love with the world. Rendering the prayer of Saint Francis of Assisi in the plural, "Lord, make us instruments of your peace."*

Inspiration

Inspiration may be defined as "divine guidance or influence exerted directly on a human mind or soul."[42] Another word with the same idea is *enthusiasm*, which comes from Latin and Greek words meaning "to be inspired by a god" or, in short, to be "in God" (*en-*, in + *theos*, god).[43] This is where, or rather from whom, we as Christ followers get our passion, our zeal, our chutzpah, our courage, and our energy! Think back to the time when the Israelites had no direction or guidance. "In those days Israel had no king; all the people did whatever seemed right in their own eyes" (Judg. 17:6 NLT). They were not inspired to live for the glory of God but were motivated by their own selfish desires. Today, we see this same dynamic at work whenever we turn on the television and watch one of the many "reality" shows where people display the nature of their selfish desires, blatantly and unapologetically satisfying them for the world to see, while polluting the minds and hearts of those who watch.

The difference is that we, as Christians, have a King who gives us direction and guidance for living an abundant life and accomplishing the purpose for which we were created. But in order to be directed and guided, we need to open our ears, to listen to what He's saying to us, and then to do it: "All Scripture is inspired by God and is useful to teach us what is true and to make us realize what is wrong in our lives. It corrects us when we are wrong and teaches us to do what is right" (2 Tim. 3:16 NLT).

For most of us, the problem is not that we lack faith in God but that we lack the knowledge to keep inspired, even as some who profess faith in Christ live with a divided heart that is not fully surrendered to Him. Jesus says, "Whoever wants to be my disciple must deny themselves and take up their cross daily and follow me" (Luke 9:23). To make the switch from being motivated to being inspired, we need to change our view of the human body and its relationship to God. As one children's book title puts it, *Jesus Wants All of Me*.[44] We need to utilize the knowledge that He gives us through His

Word and implement this knowledge in our lives. *Again, any lasting change must come from God.*

God's Desire to Be with Us

It has always been God's desire to live among us and even within us. From the very beginning He strolled through the garden with Adam and Eve in the cool of the day. He gave Moses specific instructions for building a tabernacle and later did the same with David for the temple, all because He longed to dwell among His people. Then He sent the ultimate Tabernacle—Jesus.

Jesus walked among His people. He dwelled with us; He loved us; He was right here on earth walking among us. His body was His tabernacle enfolding the presence of God within our midst.

When the Tabernacle (the Word made flesh) ascended back into heaven, what replaced it? Incredible as this may sound, *you and I* became the tabernacle! Our Lord is here with (and in) us always, just as He promised (Matt. 28:20), dwelling in His sacred tabernacles; He is within every one of us who believes and thus belongs to Him. But do we truly accept Him daily? One of the reasons that He's dwelling *within* us is so He can be *with* us. We do not have to go somewhere to be in His presence. We don't have to travel to Jerusalem or some other religious city or holy temple to be with Him.

At the beginning of the age to come, when perhaps the best way to describe it is to say that heaven comes down to earth, God's desire, expressed repeatedly in His covenants, will finally be fulfilled: "And I heard a loud voice from the throne saying, 'Behold, the dwelling place of God is with man. He will dwell with them, and they will be his people, and God himself will be with them as their God'" (Revelation 21:3 ESV).

Think of the internet, or of the chain letters and the "forwards" that allow them to go "viral." If we focus on Christ, alive within us, and allow Him to affect our hearts, we can spread His Word much more effectively. We can be like the internet and pass His message of love to all of our contacts. We too need to go viral!

We are not a mistake, and it is not a mistake that we are living at this time and in this place. In the words of Mordecai to Esther in a time of danger, "Who knows but that you have come to your royal position for such a time as this?" (Esther 4:14). Who knows indeed? He knows! In a number of ways it's true that we are living in a modern-day Persia, or perhaps worse, Rome, where people in general are worshiping many gods and living lives of overindulgence, greed, and sexual promiscuity (on national TV, nonetheless). Any student of history knows that Rome declined and fell internally long before the barbarians sacked the city in the fifth century. Twenty-first-century postmodern, post-Christian, pagan America is our time and place in which to live our lives, but we are here to serve Him, and we are here for a purpose. *We can live in the world and make it our home, but we do not have to be of the world in the sense of living as its people do (John 17:14–15).* This is an ethical distinction, not a question about the goodness God has invested into the creation, including our physical bodies. We are meant to be holy temples for God, and we owe it to Him to care for and optimize these temples for His use.

Jesus said, "All who love me will do what I say. My Father will love them, and we will come and make our home with each of them" (John 14:23 NLT). This basically tells us that if we listen to His words, His Father will come and dwell among us, *to live inside of us.* Think about that the next time you fight the temptation to hit the snooze button instead of getting up for that early morning exercise. Think about that the next time you are tempted to act out in anger and give in to sin. Think about that the next time you decide to self-medicate with recreational drugs or even junk food (more on this in chapter 7). Maybe a re-envisioned version of Robert Munger's booklet *My Heart, Christ's Home,*[45] for purposes of this book, could have us imagine Jesus waiting not only in the living room of our lives but also down in the basement, sitting on an exercise ball, suited up and ready to go; next to us giving words of encouragement not to act out in anger; or seated at our dinner table!

"For you were bought at a price," explains Paul, "so glorify God in your body *and* spirit, which are God's" (1 Cor. 6:20 NKJV, emphasis added). Note that this doesn't say just in spirit; it says in body. Our physical bodies are mentioned many times in the Bible. Our faith is the most important part of our relationship with God, but we should not neglect the body. In Mathew 6:33 Jesus says, "But seek first his kingdom and his righteousness, and all these things will be given to you as well." Seeking His kingdom is done through exercising our faith in Jesus Christ, who said of Himself, "I am the way and the truth and the life. No one comes to the Father except through me" (John 14:6).

Scripture makes clear that our priority is to be our faith, but as Christians we must not neglect His temple, the vessel that is our body. And yet we do so often tend to do just that as we live in today's culture. We need the encouragement that God gives us in His Word: "And if the spirit of Him who raised Jesus from the dead is living in you, He who raised Christ from the dead will also give life to your mortal bodies because of His Spirit who lives in you" (Rom. 8:11). We are always willing to accept the gift of life given to us, but are we always principled and conscientious about nurturing that gift, developing it, and dedicating it daily to our Creator?

Training to Be God's Look-Alikes for Now and Forever

Are you thinking at this point, "Well, our bodies are mortal; we're going to die"? This is absolutely true (unless, of course, Jesus returns first). If you are thinking this, you are not alone. I have heard many people voice some variation on the following: "We're all going to die sometime, and we may as well have fun in the process!" My response: "How much fun are you going to have when you've trashed the body you've been blessed with so badly that you have a hard time doing and enjoying daily activities? How much fun will it be to sit on the sidelines and not fulfill your purpose in life?" We are all vessels created in His likeness, placed here to do God's work for Him . . . and *someday we're going to die.* Our present mortal bodies are not going to live on. They are not going to go beyond this earthly existence. I believe this is what the apostle is referring to when he says, "I declare to you, brothers, that flesh and blood cannot inherit the kingdom of God" (1 Cor. 15:50).

So what does live on? Our spirit? Yes, the disembodied, immaterial aspect of us survives death, but that's an unnatural and temporary state for any human being to be in.[46] Actually, what will live on into the age to come is the whole enchilada: a re-embodied soul/spirit or a re-inspired/re-ensouled resurrection body—the Humpty Dumpty back together again, except that it will be new and improved, assuming you have put your hope in Christ. Paul fleshed this out for people in his day who had questions about this: "When the perishable has been clothed with the imperishable, and the mortal with immortality, then the saying that is written will come true: 'Death has been swallowed up in victory'" (1 Cor. 15:54). For those who would believe on Christ Jesus and receive eternal life, what else can we say except "Now to the King eternal, immortal, invisible, the only God, be honor and glory for ever and ever. Amen"? (1 Tim. 1:16-17).

It's pretty clear that our spirit and our faith are important and should be our first priorities as followers of Christ. Yet in keeping with a holistic approach to health and life, it's really a both/and, not an either/or. First Timothy 4:6–7 maintains the right tension, rightly elevating matters of the heart and spirit, while avoiding the Greek philosophical tendency to disparage the body: "Train yourself to be godly [e.g., in character and conduct through exercise and the practice of spiritual disciplines]. For physical training is of some value, but godliness has value for all things, holding promise for both the present life and the life to come."

What Jesus told the Pharisees concerning the tithing of spices versus the weightier matters of justice, mercy, and faithfulness applies in principle here, and it affirms the

Hebrew view of humanity, as over against the Greek view: "These you ought to have done, without neglecting the others" (Matt. 23:23). Training to be godly, to be like Jesus—that's what we need to focus on; but at the same time, how faithful, how spiritual can we be if we're neglecting His body—God's greatest creation? A patient once said to me, "I got so sick from binging on junk food after the holidays I had to apologize to my children, because I yelled at them really bad. The love of Christ wasn't coming out of me on that day. They did nothing major, but I got so angry and I just lost my patience because I wasn't feeling good."

Integrating body and soul/spirit, the apostle Paul in Romans 12:1 issues a clear call to action: "Therefore, I urge you, brothers and sisters, in view of God's mercy, to offer your bodies as a living sacrifice, holy and pleasing to God—this is your true and proper worship." When we think of what He has done for us, is this too much to ask?

What has He done for us? *He died for us.* He took off His sinless robe of righteousness and substituted it for what? For our foul, sin-stained robe. We now own that robe of His—the robe of righteousness He purchased it for us by dying for our sins. We possess it. But we've got to wear it on a daily basis, not just when we recognize that we need Him. He died for all of our sins so we could have His righteousness and return through His grace to restored fellowship with our Father in heaven.

Someday there will be no need for temples any longer. Do you know why? The apostle John tells us,

> I did not see a temple in the city, because the Lord
> God Almighty and the Lamb are its temple. The city

does not need the sun or the moon to shine on it, for the glory of God gives it light, and the Lamb is its lamp. The nations will walk by its light, and the kings of the earth will bring their splendor into it. On no day will its gates ever be shut, for there will be no night there. The glory and honor of the nations will be brought into it. Nothing impure will ever enter it, nor will anyone who does what is shameful or deceitful, but only those whose names are written in the Lamb's book of life. (Rev. 21:22–26)

God gives us quite a vision of the future. It's important, though, for us to distinguish between that celestial space described in Revelation and our place of residence once God comes to dwell forever with his people on a new earth with a new heaven (Rev. 21:1–3). Perhaps Belinda Carlisle, the lead singer of The Go-Gos, had it correct; maybe "heaven is a place on earth" after all. Until we find ourselves in glory, we are to live a life sacrificially submitted to our Father in heaven, in spite of living in today's society, which so readily embraces greed and overindulgence of our own personal desires. Giving in to the prevalent temptations of our culture will lead to a life that is displeasing to our Creator in that it systematically destroys His workmanship—our bodies, His temple. I forewarned you, didn't I, that this isn't your typical health book? Hang in there because the fun is about to begin!

What I'm saying is for everyone to embrace, but in particular we who are Christians need to rely upon God's inspiration to fuel and energize our lives with a holy enthusiasm that will make us stand out from the crowd and be His sanctuary, His *miqdash*. Together let's live a life that is pleasing to our Father as a way of proper worship, broadcasting our gratitude for the sacrifice He made for us as we share His love to the ends of the earth.

CHAPTER 3

Ruined Temples

"If I didn't work as hard as I knew I could,
then I think it would be a little bit like saying, '
God, thanks for giving me this ability, I don't really care
about it. I'm going to do something else,
and I'm not going to work quite as hard.'"

Tim Tebow, *Through My Eyes*

"Offer your bodies as living sacrifices,
holy and pleasing to God."

Romans 12:1

So far, we have discovered that we are a creation and that we have a Creator. We have studied the ancient tabernacle and temple. We have pursued many aspects of God's purpose for our bodies and how the metaphor of a temple has something to do with God's desires and the longing of the creation itself, including us as His creatures. We now have the understanding that our bodies house the Holy Spirit, both individually and collectively as the church. The church, meaning the body made up of all believers of

Christ, is to live, move, and have its being in God, according to His Word and purpose: "You are the body of Christ and each one of you is part of it" (1 Cor. 12:27). Some of the information we are about to cover will fly in the face of some of our current beliefs, and a number of us may even feel convicted, if not offended. I know I feel guilty for my failure to live out everything I say I believe is true, but God knows all this and still continues to faithfully love and forgive those who humble themselves and call on Him for grace and strength to keep on going. My prayer is that as you read the words God has put on my heart to share with you, you will reflect on how they impact you, His loved one, as well as Christ's corporate body—the church.

Our Cultural Captivity and the Unhealthy Lifestyle We Lead

We are living in an increasingly secular and post-Christian, pagan culture, where the population as a whole is focused on earthly riches and not the eternal riches promised to us from God, such as the free gift of eternal life (Rom. 6:23; John 10:27–28); peace or *shalom* (John 14:27, Rom. 5:1; Gal. 5:22; Col. 3:15); the supplying of our every need (Phil. 4:19); victory over temptation (1 Cor. 10:13); and that in all things God works for the good of those who love Him (Rom. 8:28).

Our society is perpetually striving to collect massive amounts of money for personal use and has created a culture of unprecedented greed, where people will do anything to make a quick buck. All this is led by a marketing industry that is constantly telling us we need the latest and greatest new thing. Newness is an American cultural value, and it fosters the concept of discontentment. In contrast, God's Word says that "godliness with contentment is great gain" (1 Tim. 6:6). Thus, this discontentment has led to an enormous amount of sin in today's culture, where people are marketed to in a way that says, "It is okay to be all about you, so go ahead and fulfill all your pleasures and desires." This type of marketing has bred a fear-based culture of self-absorbed people who will do anything to satisfy their earthly desires and act on things that provide instant gratification and a quick fix to eliminate whatever problem ails them.

Let's ask ourselves a few questions: What do you suppose God sees, in today's culture, when He looks at your body as a place for His Holy Spirit to live in? What do you think He might see when he looks at the body of Christ on earth— the church? What condition do you think it is in? I cannot answer what He might be seeing in your individual body, but I do believe I can shed some light on what He might be seeing in His creation around the world, based on what's going on in North America.

Specifically in North America, 76 percent of the population self-identify as Christians.[47] When I speak about the general population, due to the high percentage of proclaimed Christians, I believe we can apply many trends to the body of the church (remember, all of us together who are in Christ make up this body).

What does He see? He sees a generation that will not outlive the next. He sees His temple being destroyed by poor lifestyle choices with regard to diet and exercise. He sees more people willingly destroying their bodies by smoking cigarettes. He sees adults and teens turning toward drugs and alcohol to calm their worries and drown their sorrows. He sees more children bearing children as they ignore His word of warning against premarital sex. He sees an increase in abortion and an increasing disregard for human life from conception (abortifacients) to death (euthanasia). He sees human trafficking and the miserable sex slaves not only in the Far East but all around the world. He sees church leaders and fathers addicted to pornography. He sees adultery being committed among His people, children caught in the crossfire, and families dismembered and destroyed. He sees the orphans and widows, the marginalized and discarded, the poor and helpless, the abused and grief-stricken, the lowest of the lowest caste. He sees groups of people purposely starving themselves to obtain the super-slim figure, air-brushed model appearance that presently dominates Western concepts of feminine beauty and is broadcast continually by the mainstream media.

The point is, He sees a lot of ungodly, self-destructive acts being committed in a country historically much influenced by Christian principles, not to mention a lot of Enlightenment thinking. But with the decline of modernism and the transition into a developing postmodern era, Western civilization in general and the United States in particular have very much shifted into a post-Christian cultural pattern that witnesses increasing paganism (one who has little or no religion and who delights in sensual pleasures and material goods), as well as the despair of nihilism (from Latin *nihil,* "nothing"), "an approach to philosophy that holds that human life is meaningless and that all religions, laws, moral codes, and political systems are thoroughly empty and false."[48] On that cheery note, here are some harsh facts:

- *In 2010 The US ranked forty-ninth out of fifty-one countries* in terms of life expectancy."[49] Thus we are dying prematurely and cutting short our usefulness to God.

- Obesity + physical inactivity = 407,000 deaths per year, or approximately 17 percent of all deaths.[50] People are becoming slothful, and God warns against slothfulness. "The sluggard craves and gets nothing, but the desires of the diligent are fully satisfied" (Prov. 13:4).

- Per year, 1,051,000 deaths can be attributed to poor dietary choices. That's 45 percent of all deaths per year.[51] While Christians are not necessarily sinning by making poor food choices, since the Bible says that nothing that a man puts into his body is unclean (Matt. 7:15), we are saved by God's grace, through faith in Jesus Christ. The church in Jerusalem determined that Gentiles are no longer bound to the Mosaic laws, as the people of Israel were by virtue of God's covenant with them (Acts 15). Thus we are not sinning by eating pork, bottom feeders, or even a Twinkie. Jesus made it clear that nothing a man puts into his mouth is unclean (Mark 7:15; Matt. 15:11; 1 Tim. 4:3–5). However, the Bible also says "Everything is permissible, but not everything is beneficial" (1 Cor. 10:23). Paul wrote this to the Corinthian believers, who were struggling within their corrupt and sinful cultural environment, as they felt pressure to adapt to the ways of their society. God, in the book of Leviticus, clearly defined what is to be considered food. But the statistic introducing this bullet point indicates that many people are conforming to the fast-paced lifestyle of our current culture, without giving thought to the things they put into their body. Thus we succumb to the marketing pressures and ingest "junk food," "fast food," "energy drinks," and worse. We do not have to conform to this way of eating and drinking, since they are not proving to be beneficial and are in fact tearing down God's temple, the human body. However, we are not to shun and look down upon those who do. We can set a good example to follow, but we are responsible for our own actions, as it is aptly stated in 1 Corinthians 10:31: "So whether we eat or drink or whatever you do, do it all for the glory of God." More on this in chapter 7.

- Smoking is responsible for approximately 20 percent of all deaths per year in the US.[52] I have yet to meet a smoker who does not know that smoking is bad for them. People know it is destroying God's temple and are willingly doing it multiple times a day. Even Christians say "It's an addiction and I can't quit." I boldly say they lack in faith, as God's Word says, "I can do everything through Christ, who gives me strength" (Phil. 4:13 NLT). Granted, quitting may not be easy, but it only has to be possible. And even "impossible" things are possible with God (Matt. 19:26).

- Seventy percent of all alcohol-related deaths happen to men in general, Christians and non-Christians.[53] These men are the very ones who are called to be the leaders of their households and lead by example and teaching, according to God's Word (1 Tim. 3:1–13; Titus 2:1–2, 6–8; 5:5–9; Eph. 5:25–33; 6:4; 1 Peter 3:7). Some accept God's calling to be the leader of their household, while others do not; either way, I find alcohol abuse sad because this statistic shows a lack of self-control and leadership among men for the younger generations who follow. More on this in chapter 4.

- In the United States, three million teens between the ages of 14 and 17 are problem drinkers.[54] A problem drinker is defined as someone who becomes intoxicated at least once a month. It has been estimated that teenagers today consume 30 percent more alcohol each year than the teens of thirty years ago. Whether this intoxication is done to escape relationship problems or just to have "fun," this statistic reveals to me that they are not valuing their lives, nor having reverence for God's Word or vision for life.

- In 2009, 20 percent of US high school students had taken a prescription drug, such as Oxycontin, Percocet, Vicodin, Adderall, Ritalin, or Xanax, without a doctor's prescription.[55] Teens are doing this, instead of illicit drug use, to experience a "high" where they have a great emotional experience and feel outside their body. No matter how one justifies it, this "false" high will always produce negative consequences. We can have great emotional experiences with the Holy Spirit living inside us without destroying the vessel God has given us through which to worship Him.

- Teens also misuse over-the-counter cough and cold medications containing the cough suppressant dextromethorphan (DXM) to get high.[56]
- Three out of ten girls in the United States become pregnant at least once before age twenty. In 2006, 59 percent resulted in live birth, 27 percent resulted in abortion, and 14 percent resulted in fetal loss.[57]
- Fifty-one percent of pastors say cyber-porn is a possible temptation. Thirty-seven percent say it is a current struggle. Forty-seven percent of Christians surveyed said pornography is a major problem in their home.[58]
- In a recent Barna study, 4 out of 10 Americans said they believe that adultery is morally acceptable. For Christians, that number was 1 out of 10. Additionally, one spouse being unfaithful will impact more than 50 percent of all marriages.[59]
- The death rate associated with anorexia is twelve times higher than the death rate for all other causes of death for females 15–24 years old.[60]

With the knowledge of these shocking statistics, we can clearly see that, indeed, we are living in a self-oriented, self-serving, and very self-destructive culture. A culture of greed, excess, and an "all about me" attitude has crept its way into the church and is affecting younger and older generations, as well as causing damage to us physically, chemically, emotionally, and spiritually.

Putting Humpty Dumpty Together Again

The human body and its parts are a unit. But many of us, like Humpty Dumpty, have broken bodies that need to be put back together again. Some of us are like the woman with the twelve-year bleeding problem who before she reached out by faith to touch the edge of Jesus' cloak and was healed, the Gospel narrator says, "had suffered a great deal under the care of many doctors and had spent all she had, yet instead of getting better she grew worse" (Mark 5:26). When we get sick and stay sick, we become a puzzling mess of problems and become a mystery to our doctors. We go to the doctor, get some tests run, and are informed of the results. The doctor makes a diagnosis, writes a prescription, and we start taking some pills to deal with our presenting symptoms.

But the problem is that our health is breaking or is already broken, and the band-aid approach of symptom suppression won't make us whole again or restore us to a full measure of health unless we identify the root cause of the problems as much as is possible and deal with those problems, often by making necessary lifestyle changes. Yes, this is rather oversimplified, but the basic approach is not. Chronic illness and hereditary diseases are even more challenging to deal with, but thankfully today there are more possibilities for treatment and new therapies that aim toward restoring right function in the body. Such interventions, as well as preventative measures, are what healthcare in the future needs to be much more about.

In chapter 1, I mentioned that our bodies have three components: physical, chemical, and emotional. The physical component is comprised of our bones, muscles, organs, connective tissues, etc. The chemical component consists of blood, hormones, cytokines, neurotransmitters, vitamins and minerals etc. The emotional component is comprised of the thoughts we think, conscious and unconscious, as well as the state of our mind, which is directly influenced by our own will and spirit or by God's will and Spirit (see chapter 6). The Bible says, "the mind controlled by the Spirit is life and peace" (Rom. 8:6).

If you recall, earlier I gave an analogy of speeding down the highway and seeing a police officer with his radar gun pointed right at you. The police officer looks you in the eye— you know you are in trouble, your heart starts to pound, and your leg muscles tighten up. I used this example to demonstrate that our body is integrated such that any one part is dependent on the others. The emotional reaction was triggered by the fear of getting a speeding ticket, which caused the release of certain chemicals (adrenaline) and thereby changed the physical aspects of your body by increasing your heart rate and causing your muscles to tense up.

The physical, chemical, and emotional aspects of the body are all connected. You cannot separate the emotions from the chemicals and not affect the physical body. If one component of the body is not functioning optimally, all components are affected. The fact that all parts of the body work as one unit is pointed out in the *Guyton and Hall Textbook of Medical Physiology*, which states, "[T]he cells of the body continue to live and function properly . . . until one or more functional systems lose their ability to contribute their share of function. When this happens, *all* the cells of the body suffer. Extreme dysfunction leads to *death*; moderate dysfunction leads to *sickness*."[61]

You can rest assured that God knew this way before we did, as Paul says in 1 Corinthians 12:21–26: "The eye cannot say to the hand, 'I don't need you!' And the head cannot say to the feet, 'I don't need you!' On the contrary, those parts of the body that seem to be weaker are indispensable, and the parts that we think are less honorable we treat with special honor. And the parts that are unpresentable are treated with special modesty, while our presentable parts need no special treatment. But God has put the body together, giving greater honor to the parts that lacked it, so that there should be no division in the body, but that its parts should have equal concern for each other. *If one part suffers, every part suffers with it; if one part is honored, every part rejoices with it*" (emphasis added).

This is true of the use of our individual spiritual gifts within the function of the church, as much as it is in the amazing, self-healing, self-regulating human body that God created. God designed every part of the body to depend upon every other part for optimal function, and when we make godly choices in life, within our abilities and means, we facilitate the ability of every aspect of our body to fire on all cylinders, so to speak, and we honor God by saying, "I'm ready, use me." There is much good to do in life, and many of the possible courses or action may seem impossible or extremely difficult and challenging. In view of obstacles and even persecution for one's allegiance to Jesus Christ, the apostle Paul prayed, "Now glory be to God! By his mighty power at work within us, he is able to accomplish infinitely more than we would ever dare to ask or hope" (Eph. 3:20 NLT).

Preparing for the Oncoming Health Crisis

We live in a nation that has been built on Christian principles, but our society is lacking when it comes to living according to those principles because many people, including some Christians, are leading selfish lifestyles of indulgence. Our most fundamental obligations and privileges as Christians are to be vessels fit for God to do His work, but we have been neglecting to reach our optimal potential for His purpose. We as the church need to turn people back to our duty to God, our Creator, which we have been neglecting for far too long.

We have a severe health crisis in America that cuts across every demographic and ethnicity, Christians and non-Christians, old and young, male and female. An epidemic of chronic lifestyle diseases, which has been brought upon us, more than we care to admit, because of this perceived need for instant gratification—through selfishness, greed, and discontentment. These realities are clearly opposite the fruit of the Spirit that every Christian is expected to bear in his or her life with God: "love, joy, peace, patience, kindness, goodness, faithfulness, gentleness, and self-control" (Gal. 5:22–23). When it comes to the physical health of the body, individually and as a church, as a physician and as a Christian I see no difference between the secular world and Christians. The lifestyle of a lot of Christians living in our culture does not represent transformed lives that are being lived in accordance with God's purpose of honoring and respecting God's temple. Remember that our bodies are His temples and we were bought at a dear price.

Instead of living a fully aligned lifestyle, according to God's plan, we overindulge in the modern conveniences of today that eventually will become our postmodern inconveniences of tomorrow. We are witnessing an exponential rise in fatigue, depression, and people dying early of chronic lifestyle diseases. Do you think this impacts the way we interact with people on behalf of God? It absolutely does!

In this self-centered society in which we live, it might surprise you when I say we should not eat to be thin or exercise to look fit; our thoughts should not be for personal gain. Our focus should be on a godly life—it is *not* about how we *look* but *about how we live*. The best reason to become healthy (eating right, exercising, and thinking positively) is so that when we interact with people while living out God's purpose in our life, we have a better spirit, better endurance, and better strength to live and love and serve. Our drive should not be for our own gain (*or weight loss*), but rather for the glory of God. We should take care of our bodies in order that we may honor and glorify Him in all our actions! His honor and glory are exalted when we as Christians choose godly actions in accordance with principles laid out for us in His Word.

We need to dig deeply and truly discover how we think, how we eat, and how we move while we are stewards of the Lord's dwelling place. We do not need to build a temple for God; He has already built the temple. Our job is about stewardship and maintaining or repairing the temple that God has given to us. We need to learn to present our body on a daily basis to God, to serve Him, and to allow our body to be His dwelling place so we can spread His Word and accomplish His purpose. We need to refocus how we look at our body in relationship to God and eliminate the "Acquired

Immunity to the Bright Shining Object Syndrome" (the *lack* of awe and wonder at nature and the human body as the divine work of God's miraculous creation). Are you praising Him, thanking Him for your body, and honoring Him by caring for His amazing temple?

We also need to think about health and healing in more than just individual terms; we must use our God-given creative abilities to image the ways in which God nourishes our health and heals His people within local church congregations. We need to focus as well on the broader community of God's people, on how that can splash over in wonderful ways to those on the outside, as it did in the early days of the apostles, as recorded in several instances in the early days of the church (Acts 3–4 5:12–16). What if people outside the church looked to the church as a place of prayer and healing and wholeness instead of seeing us as the only group that sometimes shoots its own wounded? We need to get our own house to imagine what truly holistic health (physically and spiritually) can look like in a broader social context.[62] Listen to what essayist, farmer, and ecologist Wendell Berry has to say about health in this regard:

> Health, as we may remember from at least some of the days of our youth, is at once wholeness and a kind of unconsciousness. Disease (dis-ease), on the contrary, make[s] us conscious not only of the state of our health but of the division of our bodies and our world into parts.
>
> The word "health," in fact, comes from the same Indo-European root as "heal," "whole," and "holy." To be healthy is literally to be whole; to heal is to make

whole. I don't think mortal healers should be credited with the power to make holy. But I have no doubt that such healers are properly obliged to acknowledge and respect the holiness embodied in all creatures, or that our healing involves the preservation in us of the spirit and the breath of God.

If we were lucky enough as children to be surrounded by grown-ups who loved us, then our sense of wholeness is not just the completeness in ourselves but also is the sense of belonging to others and to our place. . . .

I believe that the community—in the fullest sense: a place and all its creatures—is the smallest unit of health and that to speak of the health of an isolated individual is a contradiction in terms.[63]

It's clear that as individual Christians we struggle with overcoming our own selfish desires, so often enflamed by the convenience afforded by technological innovation, and that our good intentions to dedicate our body, our time, and our lives to the glory of God get lost in the rat race of our high-speed, super-sized, anonymous, and self-ruling culture. But so does the church at large—we're captives to our culture and its values and thus very often at odds with God's name (character), kingdom (primary allegiance to Christ), and will (moral law and purpose). We need (and have!) a new Moses to deliver us from our cultural bondage: His name is Jesus ("he saves").

All of us were bought at a price to glorify God in body and spirit, so taking care of our bodies for the glory of God is important to our relationship with Him. We need to get better at caring for His creation, these human vessels, as a way to honor and worship Him. And that includes seeing people as part of their communities and seeing ourselves as members of one another in the body of Christ, the church, which our Lord redeemed by His blood. The apostle Peter reminds us of this collective emphasis in the metaphor of a house, which is essentially the purpose served by the temple Solomon built:[64] "As you come to him, the living Stone—rejected by men but chosen by God and precious to him—you also, like living stones, are being built into a spiritual house to be a holy priesthood, offering spiritual sacrifices acceptable to God through Jesus Christ" (2 Peter 2:4–5).

If God did not view lightly the misuse of His vessels of gold and silver and the disrespect for life during the time of the Babylonian empire, do you believe He will be casual about the shameless abuse of His church and temple, our body, today by the world, the flesh, and the devil? (Eph. 2:2–3).

Christian or non-Christian, we are all human beings, a work of God's creative effort, bearers of the divine image, destined to participate or share in the divine nature through our union with Christ (2 Peter 1:4). Let's not wait for the proverbial or prophetic "handwriting on the wall" to tell us that this generation has been weighed on the divine scales of judgment and found wanting! Let's get intentional and knowledgeable on the care of His vessel, because our actions affect not only this generation but also the generations to come.

CHAPTER 4

Generations

"Why are we witnessing the forecast of a decline in life expectancy in the next generation in the face of being the most medicated society the world has ever seen?"
Jeffery Bland

*"But the plans of the L*ORD* stand firm forever, the purposes of his heart through all generations."*
Psalm 33:11

"If the church marries herself to the spirit of the times, she will find herself a widow in the next generation."
Charles Stanley

Have you ever seen a family where the grandparents, parents, and children all have given their lives in service to their fellow man? Where the different generations of the same family all became doctors, teachers, military men and women, farmers, firefighters, police officers, pastors, youth leaders, missionaries, etc.? Or even generational families that seem to be successful no matter what they do?

How about the not so bright side? Have you ever seen a family where the father has uncontrollable anger and his son seems to have it as well? Have you ever seen the congregation of a church have an epidemic of generational adultery, where the parents commit adultery with their peers, and then years later their children do the same thing within the same congregation? Have you ever seen families who all seem to be obese, from the grandparents to the grandchildren? How about generations of criminals in the same family?

I have witnessed every one of these tendencies, the good and the bad, and I'll bet that you can relate to some of these as well. Families can pass many things down from generation to generation. The family is God's idea from the very beginning. Its members are to offer unconditional love, honor, and respect to each other. It is important to note that when something happens to one family member, all are affected one way or another. This can have positive and negative impacts. *Any generation has the ability to change the direction of the generational line for the good or for the bad.*

Jesus was descended from Rahab the harlot (prostitute), who made a change when she chose to hide the Israelite spies. God blessed her and her entire family down through her generations (read her story in Joshua 2 and 6 and note her legacy in the story of Ruth, especially 4:13–22; also note Heb. 11:31 and James 2:25). This is in stark contrast to King Nebuchadnezzar's generational line mentioned in chapter 2. Nebuchadnezzar took the gold and silver vessels from the temple in Jerusalem before destroying it (Dan. 1:1–2). Then years later his son, Belshazzar, continued the abuse and misuse of God's temple belongings by using the silver and gold in the feast, resulting in the fall of the Babylonian empire (Dan. 5).

First Timothy 5:4 talks about the family as the place where spiritual nurturing begins. The parents have the responsibility of showing their children the importance of a spiritual life and training them in godliness. A great example of this spiritual nurturing is seen in 2 Timothy 1:5, where we read, "I am reminded of your sincere faith, which first lived in your grandmother Lois and in your mother Eunice and, I am persuaded, now lives in you also." Eunice's faith was passed down from her grandmother Lois, and Eunice in turn passed it down to her son Timothy. You can see in this passage the importance that each generation has with each other as one generation is influenced by the generation ahead and they influence the generation behind, as each generation is directly linked to the other two.

Here is the point: we are living in unprecedented times in history where researchers are forecasting a decline in the life expectancy of this youngest generation, in spite of being the most medicated society the world has ever seen.[65] Let's look at three examples of generational, environmental changes that have influenced this current young population to have a lower life expectancy than their parents. We are going to look at one example from each category of stressors to which the human body responds: emotional stress, chemical stress, and physical stress.

Emotional Stress

In the 1950s through the 1970s, children's blood pressure readings were stable from birth to about age six, with an average systolic blood pressure reading of 100 mmHg. Generally speaking, this was at a time in history when mothers were at home raising the children while the fathers worked. However, after age six children's blood pressure would start to gradually rise, so that by the time they were seventeen years old their systolic blood pressure would be about 130 mmHg. What occurred at age six that caused the blood pressure to start rising? The child was delivered from their mother's protection and care and given to the care and protection of strangers—in other words, *school*. This can create a lot of emotional stress for a child, affecting their physiology. However, in today's society, mothers are shifting away from the care of their infants and moving into the workplace. As a result, we are observing that blood pressures are beginning to rise in the first year of life instead of age six, according to the National Institutes of Health 1997.[66]

This affects our generations, because increased blood pressure is second on the list of preventable risk factors for *premature death* in the United States. High blood pressure is a contributing factor for the number one killer among Americans, heart disease.[67] I present this information not to condemn or to criticize mothers who work; please do not feel that you are necessarily harming your child because you work outside the home. My point is to show that our actions and behaviors impact not only ourselves but the whole family in ways that we may never have imagined. If we are made aware that emotional stressors affect our physiology, we will then at least have the ability to help counteract our body's negative adaptation (e.g., rising blood pressure) to various emotional stressors that occur in daily life.

Chemical Stress

One hundred years ago we did not have the prevalence of the chronic lifestyle diseases that we do today. This is in large part due to the food we choose to eat. One hundred years ago we did not have fast food at every stop along the way, nor calorie-rich, nutrient-depleted packaged foods that are laden with manmade, synthetic, sometimes toxic preservatives, and way too much refined sugar. Nor did we have the widespread use of pesticides and herbicides on our produce that we have today. These chemicals have detrimental effects on the health of the human body—God's temple.

Proverbs 23:1–3 says, "When you sit to dine with a ruler, note well what is set before you, and put a knife to your throat if you are given to gluttony. Do not crave his delicacies, for that food is deceptive." I don't believe these verses are necessarily referring to the food as much as to the lifestyle. We need to maintain daily nutrition and stand firm within healthy boundaries. During the time and place that the book of Proverbs was written, it was only the rulers and dignitaries who regularly ate rich foods like pastries, wine and beer, lots of animal meat, fat, and the like. The commoners didn't have access to rich foods but survived eating vegetables, grains, fruit, and wild game when they could hunt or trap it. Consequently, it was only the wealthy who contracted the ailments that became known as "the diseases of kings and queens." What were those diseases? Arthritis, cancer, obesity, heart disease, and other chronic lifestyle illnesses that were largely unknown among commoners.

In modern America almost everyone eats calorie-rich, nutrient-depleted foods, and as a consequence we are an entire nation of people who suffer from the diseases of kings and queens. Researchers are forecasting a decline in the life expectancy of the next generation, because currently the children born of the late 1980s and 1990s grew up eating high-calorie, nutrient-depleted foods, and when as adults they attempt to conceive a baby there is not an optimal environment to foster the proper fetal growth and development. As a result we are seeing an increasing number of women who are having fertility issues, due in part to the chemical stressors put on the body by the environment in which a person breathes, eats, drinks, and lives. This will adversely affect the generation's lineage and not allow this generation to optimally fulfill God's command to "be fruitful and increase in number; fill the earth and subdue it" (Gen. 1:28).

As for the children born from mothers of that generation, 60 percent are considered overweight or obese before puberty, and we no longer use the term "adult onset diabetes" because we have an epidemic number of children being diagnosed with this condition, which is now termed "Type II Diabetes." This condition leads to an increased risk of many other lifestyle diseases that debilitate people's health and shorten their life spans, thus minimizing our participation in fulfilling God's purpose for our lives. It is evident throughout the Bible that God can use anyone, but do we want merely to be used, or do we prefer to be useful?

Physical Stress

As mentioned in an earlier chapter, today's modern conveniences are becoming tomorrow's inconveniences, as many of us are less physically active in our day-to-day life, due in no small measure to technology that automates many human functions and thus limits our physical movement. This next statement is going to come across as a contradiction, but stay with me: a lack of physical stress on our body actually causes physical stress on our body, because a lack of movement will cause degeneration in our joints and bones. The fact of the matter is that our body was made to move. Research says, "Evidence shows beyond reasonable doubt that *immobilization* (lack of movement) is not only a cause of osteoarthritis but that it delays healing."[68]

Osteoarthritis creates a domino effect as it increases physical stress due to altered biomechanics. As a result, it increases chemical stress via systemic bodily inflammation, which in turn leads to chronic pain that will then increase emotional stress since chronic pain has been proven to lead to depression. In 2009 Harvard public health researchers published an article delineating the leading *preventable* risk factors for *premature death* in the United States, and inadequate physical activity or inactivity was number four on the list.[69] Imagine how inactive this next generation will be if we don't lead by example and be intentional about using our bodies the way they were created to move.

Closing the Generation Gap

These are three of the many examples in the health field of lifestyle factors that are leading to a decrease in the life expectancy of the next generation. We are engendering a slow but steady trend toward diminished health and vitality in life, shorter life spans, and premature death in the general population. Give the church's captivity to North American culture, which is evident in so many ways, we might as well conclude that our lifestyle preferences are promoting early extinction among God's people rather than encouraging them to lead lives that are fully aligned with God's Word in every area, including healthy living. What I fear the most is that we will repeat history. In Judges 2:10 we read, "After that whole generation had been gathered to their ancestors, another generation grew up who knew neither the LORD nor what He had done for Israel." As our health goes down the tube, so our spiritual vitality can be drained to the point of impotence.

As a general observation I would posit that members of today's younger generation don't seem to care about themselves enough to do something about their future or that of the generations to follow. Many young people don't respect and value the older generation. In fact, in our society that values youth so highly, an entire anti-aging subculture has emerged, developing many products and programs that are little more than vain gimmicks to prevent or camouflage aging, an inevitable consequence of human sin. God put you in your current generation on purpose. He appointed each of us to fulfill His purpose in our generation, and it is our duty both to help the generation that came before us and to influence and encourage the generation behind us, who in turn will influence the generations to come. Throughout God's Word the righteous proclaim that their purpose is to declare the glory of God to the next generation: "Even when I am old and gray, do not forsake me, O God, till I declare your power to the next generation, your might to all who are to come" (Ps. 71:18). If we are to think biblically, we need to think generationally.

Here are some questions to ask yourself with regard to your circle of influence. As you read the questions below, think about the lifestyle you lead, as well as about your behaviors and tendencies in times of stress. Think about the example you are setting for those who are watching you. Are you living a life of "do as I say, not as I do" or are you leading a fruitful and healthy life that is called according to God, so that when the day comes you will hear the words "well done, good and faithful servant?"

To those in the oldest generation:
- Are you sharing your experiences with those who are walking the same path you walked?
- Are you mentoring those younger than you?
- Are you encouraging them?
- Are you seeing the good and value in the younger generations?

To those in the middle generation:
- Are you respecting those older than you?
- Do you tap into their fountain of expertise, acknowledging that they have walked where you are now walking? Are you willing to let them mentor you?
- Are you mentoring those younger than you?
- Are you encouraging them?
- Are you seeing the good in them?
- Are you seeing that they want to live godly lives?

To those in the younger generation:
- Are you respecting those older than you?
- Are you seeking out mentors?
- Are you seeing their wisdom, knowing that they've walked your road long before you?
- Are you gleaning all you can from them?

Are you leading a godly life for the next generation to follow you?

God is the God of every generation—as He has been called "the God of Abraham, Isaac and Jacob." God says, "One generation shall praise thy works to another, and shall declare thy mighty acts" (Ps. 145:4 KJV). We can see clearly that each generation is called to build on the foundation left by its predecessors. Therefore, all generations are in great need of all others to complete the work that God has called His corporate body to fulfill.

Every generation has the chance to change the world and fulfill God's purpose, but all of us, especially our current younger generation, are shortening the chances of our future generations with the unhealthy lifestyle choices we are making. Many of these choices are a result of the influence and bondage of the previous generation. I am going to share with you a story that I have witnessed in my office as I treated a whole family. I share this story because I believe it represents at least half of our current population, with regard to the destructive generational influences, and I believe anyone with a family can relate to at least some aspects.

The father of the house comes home from a long day at a mediocre paying job that barely covers the bills, feeling less than satisfied as he feels stuck in a dead-end job that is far short of the childhood aspirations that he shared with me. The demands of his home life begin to sink in as he decompresses from his work day. Children want to play with him, his wife has projects for him to do, and all he can think about is the day's mail to sort through—stressful in itself, since most pieces are bills that need to be paid. The stress builds up; his threshold for stress is approaching the boiling point, lowered from back pain due to the labor of his job.

But just before he explodes with anger and frustration he hears an inner voice: "You have done your work today; you have worked to provide food and clothes for the family. Now it's everyone else's turn. So relax; call some friends over to hang out in the garage and drink some beer and share some smokes." He then decides to act on the voice in his head, as it is much more appealing than dealing with the realities of life, so he takes a mini vacation from reality and self-medicates his physical pain, emotional stress, and subsequent depression with alcohol, cigarettes, and marijuana.

His wife, whose overtaxed brain has barely completed a single thought during the day (having tended to the children all day long—cleaning them, feeding them, and cleaning their messes, only to do it over and over again until she feels literally insane) has waited all day long to see her husband. She looks at the clock and thinks, *It's almost 5 o'clock. "My man" should be home soon. Yes, help is on the way!* She hurries to makes one last-ditch effort to clean the house and finish dinner so he won't be stressed out when he walks through the door.

Finally, her husband shows up . . . late. The dinner has turned cold during the children's evening meltdown, and she is stressed out and feels worn and tattered. She is looking for a little help from her husband and possibly a stimulating adult conversation, but he has already checked out and is in his mental vacation land. The wife becomes sad, painfully aware that everything she has done all day long, including the last-minute preparations for his arrival, has gone unnoticed.

She now feels defeated and is searching to fill her void of emptiness. She turns to sweets and salty treats, such as ice cream, soda, chips, and candy.

This goes on for a while, but over time her body starts to become unhealthy. She is plagued by constant fatigue, aching joints, and an ever-expanding waistline. However, she continues to medicate her loneliness, depression, fatigue, and pain with comfort food. She is feeling anything but attractive for her husband, and she feels she can barely take care of herself, not to mention their children. The household chores begin to suffer, leading to an increased demand for her husband to pick up the slack. He feels the demand, but his threshold for stress is maxed out, so he avoids the issue altogether. After work he begins to frequent bars and adult clubs to hang out and instantaneously unplug from reality. This leads to bedtime arguments and abuse for the children to hear and sometimes see.

The children are being raised to idealize their parents, and soon they begin to follow suit. They start fighting and arguing with each other at home and with other kids at school. They begin to eat junk food as a staple instead of a treat, resulting in poor health and many illnesses. They are pessimistic and frequently use foul language. One of the children even begins looking at pornographic magazines with his friends in the garage—while smoking cigarettes.

What I find most interesting is that the father of this young family was once a star athlete who was sexually abused by a chronically alcoholic family member. I'll bet the family member who sexually abused the father as a child had no idea or even gave a thought to the consequences of his actions on this boy's future family. As you can see demonstrated in this story, the snowball effect of generational influence is of great magnitude, and we must perform self-audits and audits on each other, while holding each other accountable, to keep us on a godly path. Whether we know it or not, we influence people all the time, but we have to be intentional about doing it in a good and healthy way.

Research is even indicating that a mother's emotional status can influence the development of a fetus and his or her emotional tendencies outside the womb. We must be deliberate in every area of our life and not permit the future of God's temple to continue to go down the path of destruction due to selfish desires and the demands for instant gratification that continuously tug at our heart in stressful times!

Second Timothy 3:1–4 states, "But mark this: There will be terrible times in the last days. People will be lovers of themselves, lovers of money, boastful, proud, abusive, disobedient to their parents, ungrateful, unholy, without self-control, brutal, not lovers of the good, treacherous, rash, conceited, lovers of pleasure rather than lovers of God." None of us are guaranteed tomorrow, so let us make every day count for the greater good. Satan is instigating outright warfare among the generations, and the biggest bull's-eye for the devil to attack is our problems with consistency. When we're stuck on ourselves, there is a great deal of inconsistency in our walk as Christians. In order to be prepared for this battle we must know the areas in life in which we are most inconsistent. Following is a list of questions paraphrased from Scripture that will allow you to begin the self-auditing process to identify your inconsistencies and begin to strengthen your convictions, in Christ, to overcome them.

- Do you live life with a "do as I say, not as I do" mentality? (Romans 2:21–23).
- Do you judge others but exclude yourself (for example, condemning another person for something that you are guilty of doing yourself)? (Matthew 7:3).
- Do you often talk about the Christian life but fail to actually walk it? (Titus 1–16).
- When you are lonely and afflicted, to whom or what do you turn? (Psalm 25:16–17).
- Do you frequently act out in anger and do foolish things? (Psalms 37:8).
- Do you answer people in crass or insensitive ways calculated to stir up anger? (Proverbs 15:1).
- Are you using your God-given gifts to help others, which may in turn bring Him glory? (Mathew 5:16).
- Do you give abundantly of your resources to help those in need? (Proverbs 22:16).
- Do you look lustfully at others? (Mathew 5:27–28).

We must be strong in our faith, as the enemy would love nothing more than to see another person fall short of what God intends for them. Are you going to take a stand and lead the younger generation by your example to live a fully aligned and healthy life, according to God's plan? Let us be a healthy and fruitful generation that seeks Him wholeheartedly.

CHAPTER 5

Boundaries

"Boundaries are to protect life, not to limit pleasures."
Edwin Louis Cole

*"I will instruct you (says the Lord) and guide you along
the best pathway for your life; I will advise
you and watch your progress."*
Psalms 32:8 TLB

A boundary is defined as something that indicates a border or limit.[70] There are some well-known moral boundaries called universal truths. These are boundaries we know are just wrong to cross; we are not supposed to do these things, period. For example, it is wrong to murder, steal, lie, or commit adultery. We easily recognize boundaries that are related to sin. However, what is not so easy for us to see are the boundaries that are related to our gifts. These gifts can come in many forms, such as food, the elements of earth, work, spiritual gifts, technology, family, home, car, etc. God is the giver of these gifts. He gives us many wonderful gifts to enjoy; the problem is that we become enslaved to them. It is human nature, in our fallen condition, to latch onto something too tightly. That's why God gifts us with boundaries as well.

Boundaries for Our Daily Bread (Manna)

God told Moses he was to lead the Israelites out of Egypt, where they had been slaves for hundreds of years, to the Promised Land of Canaan. This was a trip that would be burdened with many difficulties, but God wanted His people, the Israelites, to know His power so that they would be strong and believe in Him when things were difficult (see, e.g., Deut. 20:1). This was an exciting time for the Israelites because God had taken them out of slavery; but it was also a scary time, as they were about to face the unknown of the desert.

Since you might not immediately recognize a slave's behavior or mentality, let me first explain what that's about. In both the physical and the spiritual sense the term "slave" refers to one who is in bondage, experiencing some form of captivity or imprisonment, limited in liberty to become free. A slave can be described as having no freedom to exercise a will of his or her own, completely under the control of another. Now imagine with me what your mentality would be like if your entire family had been slaves for centuries. You are in captivity, not knowing how much, what type, and when you are going to receive food or be given water, despite your doing everything you're commanded to do. You literally have no control of your life. Do you believe you would have a scarcity mentality, formed by your environment of captivity? I know I would. I would likely hoard food and water and capitalize whenever I could on any situation where I might have the control to make a decision.

Now imagine that you're liberated. You have the freedom to choose when and what to eat, how to spend your day, etc. Now you choose to follow your God, who has led you out of slavery into a desert. Do you believe you'd be scared? I know I would be. Knowing nothing else but slavery and having a slave's mentality, would you be free in your mind to openly trust God? God didn't want the Israelites to be free only from Pharaoh's power, his culture, and his gods; He wanted them to be walking free in His love and grace so they could worship Him without constraint. Repeatedly the message came to Pharaoh: "Let my people go, that they may serve me" (Exod. 7:16).

God gave the Israelites the great gift of food in the form of manna, but he also set some boundaries that we read about in Exodus 16:4–5: "Then the LORD said to Moses, I will rain down bread from heaven for you. The people are to go out each day and gather enough for that day. In this way I will test them and see whether they will follow my instructions. On the sixth day they are to prepare what they bring in, and that is to be twice as much as they gather on the other days."

From this passage you can see that God was teaching them boundaries. He was teaching them to be satisfied and to take only enough for that day. Notice He said "day." He did not say get enough to store up for tomorrow, which is our natural inclination. Only on the sixth day were they to collect a double portion and prepare it. Imagine you had been there yourself. Would you have gathered only enough to satisfy yourself and your family (remember that you would likely still have had the scarcity mentality of captivity)? The majority would gather more than needed.

If we look at the current trends in America, we notice a tendency in our culture to have a "feast or famine" mentality, and we too often go for the "super size." You will see in the next passage that our mentality is not much different today from what it was back then. In spite of the specific instructions God gave to them, the Israelites did not obey. We read in Exodus 16:19–20, "Then Moses said to them, 'No one is to keep any of it until morning.' However, some of them paid no attention to Moses; they kept part of it until morning, but it was full of maggots and began to smell. So Moses was angry with them."

Boundaries for Our Day of Rest and Worship

God gives us instruction for a reason, although we may not understand it. Rest assured, His instructions are always for the greater good. The whole point of them collecting a double portion and preparing it on the sixth day was so they could have food on the Sabbath, the day of rest. "Eat it today," Moses said, "because today is a Sabbath to the LORD. You will not find any of it on the ground today. Six days you are to gather it, but on the seventh day, the Sabbath, there will not be any" (Exod. 16:25–26). God did not want his people going out and collecting the manna on the day set aside to worship Him.

A break in the pattern of six days of work allows God's people in every era to set aside our pleasures, our ways, and our often idle conversation and remember with delight that the central reality of life is not work but God, whom we honor in special ways on that day (see Isa. 58:13–14). The Sabbath principle is established in the beginning of the story of Genesis, before man even chose to sin. God's instruction included His provision of food, as well as His ways for His people to work and worship.

I would like to suggest that in the book of Genesis the works of creation can be divided naturally into two parts: the creation of the domain and the creation of its inhabitants. On the first day God created day and night, on the second day he created the heavens and the sea, and on the third day he created land and vegetation. These are the dominions that the rest of His creatures are to inhabit. On the fourth day God made the sun and moon, which dwell, respectively, in the day and night that He created on day one. On day five God created the birds and the fish, which make their home, respectively, in the heavens and the sea that were created on the second day. On the sixth day God created land animals, and then he created man and woman, who are to rule over everything as they dwell in the land that was created on the third day. Now imagine you were creating all these amazing things. Wouldn't you want to just keep going?

However, we should resist the urge to keep going when it's time to stop. God knew that when a job is done, it's finished. Overdoing things would have spoiled His creation. Thus, on the seventh day God Himself rested from His work of creating the world and blessed that day, setting it apart (making it holy) as a day of rest. We have nothing less than the example of the Creator Himself to follow in resting from our work as He did. This day was also set to keep clear who is ruler over all.

What happens when we go overboard with the gifts with which God has blessed us? The very things that were supposed to be our gifts become foul. Just as with the manna, the distaste and foulness spill over into other areas of our life, spoiling the whole "batch." Have you ever heard the saying "one bad apple spoils the bunch"? As one apple rots, it affects all the other apples. The rotting starts to spread throughout the applecart, like cancer. I remember my high school football coach addressing the team with these words, "Don't be the bad apple; don't be a cancer to this team!" He was referring to our state of mind, to whether we were positive or negative, a good example or a bad example for others; to whether or not we followed the guidelines that he had laid out for the team. We had the potential to change the losing streak of a horrible football team three years in a row into something great. If we were to make a significant change, we needed to be united in the foundational principles of the team, as laid out by our leader, the coach. Not only as individuals but also collectively, as a team. One individual can take charge with a fiery spirit and lead the way for others to follow.

It is the same way with our bodies, God's temples, and with the corporate body of Christ—the church. When we choose to follow, or choose not to follow, healthy boundaries laid out by God, our actions affect the whole body. The metaphor of our human body illustrates the truth about the way the individual members of the church are to function. As the apostle Paul explained it, "If one part suffers, every part suffers with it; if one part is honored, every part rejoices with it" (1 Cor. 12:26). God gave the Israelites manna to eat, and all they had to do was go out and collect it. But due to their intractable unbelief and lack of trust (typical mentality of a slave), they spoiled God's provision and disregarded the day fasting.

God set a boundary for us to follow as well: one day each week set aside to rest, break free from our day-to-day agenda, and focus on Him. I do not believe that the Sabbath must be observed on Saturday or even Sunday as long as we are respecting the boundaries, breaking free of whatever is enslaving us and centering our attention on God.

So how about a real-life example, right? Let's take, for instance, social media. (*I know he did not just bring up social media!* you're fuming. *Now the doctor is preaching, or worse, meddling! Imagine the audacity of an author who dares to say something that messes with my lifestyle!* Well, here goes nothing, y'all.) Do you, or can you, take a break from technology and the constant incoming stream of information? Might putting the principle of this Sabbath command into practice mean no email for one day each week, no checking Facebook, no posting updates, no turning on your cell phone for at least part of the day on which you worship or during worship services, no internet, no TV, no radio, no videos or films—none of the electronic stuff we might typically do the other days of the week?

So perhaps you're wondering *Why all the restrictions?* I realize you may be saying *This sounds like slavery and legalism to me.* Rest assured. God has always graciously made allowances for works of piety (for doing good), works of mercy and charity (hauling your neighbor's ox out of a ditch), and works of necessity (putting out a house or car fire). Yet, however you view your responsibility to God and neighbor on your "sabbath," here's the real question: Is the Lord Himself the central focus of this one day of the week?

Listen to the blessing Isaiah the prophet offered to God's people of old, who evidently were not keeping God's special day at the center but knew very well from the Law that they ought to be doing so:

> "If you keep your feet from breaking the Sabbath
> and from doing as you please on my holy day,
> if you call the Sabbath a delight
> and the Lord's holy day honorable,
> and if you honor it by not going your own way
> and not doing as you please or speaking idle words,
> then you will find your joy in the Lord,
> and I will cause you to ride on the heights of the land
> and to feast on the inheritance of your father Jacob."

The mouth of the Lord has spoken. (Isa. 58:13–14 NIV)

If you struggle to know what you need to take a break from, ask this question of the thing in question: Does it control you or do you control it? The weekly day of rest is all about resisting the urge to continue doing whatever is gripping us throughout our week. Why? So we can focus on God, our Redeemer. And this is to say nothing of the health benefits associated with regular rest.

If we look at our society, we can see that we need to become intentional about finding rest in God. If we are not intentional about taking a break from whatever is enslaving us, what are we spoiling or rotting?

Boundaries for Our Work and Families

In 2008, God laid on my heart to leave my position as an associate doctor and open up my own office. I did not want to do this, as I had three young kids, had just built a new house, and I loved my job. I thought to myself, *What if the business fails? What if I cannot support my family? What if we lose our house? What if? What if? What if?* Finally, I decided to follow God's seemingly crazy plan. I walked into my house, looked at my wife, threw my arms in the air and said, "The Lord has set me free." Free I was, indeed. No income to pay my student loans or anything else, no job, no place to start my new business . . . the only things that seemed to be "free" to me were what people were giving us.

As I searched for locations for my new business, talked to banks about getting a loan, and put together my business plan, the Lord provided. Friends anonymously left groceries on my porch, gift cards were found on my car seat, people invited us over for dinner more often, a perfect business location opened up with a godly servant of a landlord, the bank loan came through, and two amazing staff members appeared. I was set to take on the world. Business was awesome; I was blessed with more than I could ever have imagined. God and His people had indeed cared for us in this time of transition. "Now all glory to God, who is able, through his mighty power at work within us, to accomplish infinitely more than we might ask or think" (Eph. 3:20). Paul says in Romans 8:28, "And we know that in all things God works for the good of those who love him, who have been called according to his purpose." I was being faithful, and I loved Him, and He provided more than I could have ever imagined.

Not wanting to disappoint God in response to His blessings, and not wanting to let my family down, I worked. I mean *worked*! I went to bed at 1:00 a.m. and woke up at 3:00 a.m.—I worked, worked, and then worked some more. I would be gone before the kids would awake in the morning and get home just before bedtime. Wanting to be the good husband and father, I would swing home for lunch for about thirty minutes before going back to work so I could feel good about myself. Of course I was there physically, but mentally I was always working. I was present, yet absent. I was doing all this as my mind became more focused on the things of this world, forgetting what God says: "It is useless to work so hard for a living, getting up early and going to bed late. For the Lord provides for those He loves, while they are asleep" (Ps. 127:2 GNT).

Can any of you relate to my situation? Even on weekends, we would hang out with the best neighbors in the world, but I would find myself mentally working and not truly being present. It was so bad my neighbors would say, "Come back to us, buddy; we're over here." Then came the last straw. I came home one night and my wife said to me, "Do you know what your son said tonight at dinner?" I responded, "No, what?" She said, "He asked if our family was going to be okay?" I asked, "Why would he say that?" to which she replied, "Because he said we never have dinner all together anymore." Talk about breaking your heart. My child thought our family was not going to be a family any longer.

You see, here was a situation in which God had blessed and I had become enslaved to the blessings. At what cost? Just as with the manna, I was spoiling my relationships and missing some cherished moments with my family and friends, the very ones whom I love. On top of that, I took God's blessing and allowed it to disrupt my fellowship with Him. I, in fact, had become enslaved to my gift and had committed the sin of gluttony, in that I allowed my gift to become my sin.

Our Freedom in Christ and Its Loving Boundaries in Life

Gluttony can be defined as greedy or excessive indulgence.[71] Gluttony does not have to be about food and alcohol; it can be about any gift we have been given. "For drunkards and gluttons become poor, and drowsiness cloths them in rags" (Prov. 23:21). When I was working my tail off and never really resting my mind, I was becoming rich with earthly things, and yet I was poor. Again, it is easy for us to see the boundaries of sin in the universal truths. How much pornography and adultery are okay? How much lying is okay? How much murder is okay? Just a little . . . No! None of it is okay. But how much work is okay? How many after-school activities for kids are okay? How much technology is okay? How much sugar is okay? How much food is okay? These are tough questions to answer, falling as they do into a less clear-cut domain, but it is even harder to recognize and apply right values to the choices we make when we have too much even of a good thing and are stuck in captivity.

When I was in school I learned an analogy about a frog that serves as a needed warning, especially to the church today. When you throw a frog into a boiling pot of water, it will immediately try to hop out of the water for survival. However, if you put the frog in water that is room temperature and slowly turn up the heat, the frog will adjust to the temperature increase and will stay in the water until it boils to death.

We can recognize sin that is outright wrong, but when we are comfortable with a particular gift God has given us, we let our guard down and start rationalizing and making exceptions. Eventually these so-called "exceptions" begin to rule our life, and we slowly cook ourselves to death without even realizing it. The enemy loves it when we give in to gluttony, as it creates a separation in our relationship with God.

"The thief comes only to steal and kill and destroy," points our Jesus. "I have come that they may have life, and have it to the full" (John 10:10). I believe this Scripture verse gives us insight as to when enough becomes too much, when something that we are habitually doing, *even if it's a good thing*, comes between us and our relationship with God. Ask yourself if what you are doing is godly? If it is, does it still impinge upon your time or energy for other godly duties, such as being a spouse or parent? If yes, then you are likely not living life to the fullest, as intended by God. Something in your life is in excess, and it is not allowing room for God in your life. Do not let anyone or anything else stand in place of God!

Resist the temptation to overindulge and commit the sin of gluttony. You are His creation, placed in a generational line, so you can change yourself and your descendants for the good. But if you don't resist, your indulgence will be for the bad. Remember what the Lord has done for you:

salvation through Christ cost God dearly; you were bought and redeemed at a great price. "It is for freedom that Christ has set us free. Stand firm, then, and do not let yourselves be burdened again by a yoke of slavery" (Gal. 5:1). "Be still, and know that I am God! I will be honored by every nation. I will be honored throughout the world" (Ps. 46:10 NLT). Honor and respect God's boundaries. Do this "with all your heart and with all your soul and with all your strength and with all your mind" (Luke 10:27), for every part of the body is interdependent and has influence on the others. The Lord's rest and blessing will be yours to enjoy as you know Him and serve Him with a life that is full of His abundance and free of whatever would entangle you.

CHAPTER 6

The Mind

*"Watch your thoughts for they become words, watch
your words for they become actions, watch your actions
for they become habits, watch your habits for they
become your character, watch your character for it
becomes your destiny. What we think we become."*
Margaret Thatcher, *The Iron Lady*

*"Let the peace of Christ rule in your hearts,
since as members of one body you were called to peace.
And be thankful."*
Colossians 3:15

It is important that we start off in this section with the understanding that the world wants to control our mind. The world wants to influence our every thought, from what we buy and when we buy to our activities (or lack of activity) of daily living. Unfortunately, the majority of this influence is intended to monopolize our minds for the financial gain of another entity, no matter what the cost. This continuous demand for control of our mind from the outside world has led to the bombardment of marketing that sends the message of fear, discontentment, and self-centeredness. We may think that we are immune to this type of influence. However, over time we will develop a hardened heart if we are not intentional about recognizing these subliminal messages of power and control. If we're not careful, without even realizing it we may end up like the frog in the kettle I mentioned in the previous chapter. Have you ever bought something because you heard or read the words "today only"? No matter how you rationalize it, the marketing got you, creating the fear of scarcity in your mind.

We have established in the previous chapters that everything about our body is interconnected and has influence over the other parts and systems. In the story of the speeding car I described the chemical and physical changes that occur when fear (an emotion) is triggered when the driver sees a police officer. This kind of emotional and bodily reaction occurs in the same manner no matter what the stressor may be in your life, whether it causes you to be happy, sad, afraid, anxious, hopeless, excited, or whatever. However, some of these emotions have a better influence over your body than others. We know that our mind controls our body . . . but what is it that controls our mind?

Spirit over Mind

The spirit controls the mind. However, in today's self-seeking, self-gratifying, self-centered, and fear-based world, many people focus on "willpower" to control their mind, and they usually fail. Letting the world control their mind thus diminishes their attempts to be Christ-like in their daily actions. "So I tell you this," declares Paul, "and insist on it in the Lord, that you must no longer live as the Gentiles do, in the futility of their thinking. They are darkened in their understanding and separated from the life of God because of the ignorance that is in them due to the hardening of their hearts. Having lost all sensitivity, they have given themselves over to sensuality so as to indulge in every kind of impurity, and they are full of greed" (Eph. 4:17–19).

When we accept Christ into our lives we are to change from within, even as the world endlessly inundates us from the outside. If we succumb to the outside pressures we will be a conformer, but if we submit to the will of God and let His will and spirit control our mind we will be a transformer—no, not one like my sons' toys. God says through Paul, "Do not conform to the pattern of this world, but be transformed by the renewing of your mind. Then you will be able to test and approve what God's will is—His good, pleasing and perfect will" (Rom. 12:2).

How do we surrender our will to God? This can be accomplished through disciplined prayer and by engrafting God's Word into our lives every day, not just on Sunday. When we pray to God we can surrender our will to Him. In the book of Matthew chapter 6, Jesus warns against being a hypocrite and praying for public display and notoriety. In this chapter Jesus also teaches His disciples what we commonly refer to as the Lord's Prayer. We do well to take note of the wording: "Your will be done"—not our will, not the world's will, but the will of God our Father be done in our lives (Matt. 6:10). Many times we think of God's overall will in our lives, but we need to focus on God's will over *all*. Literally, His will is to rule over *all*—all our thoughts, desires, and actions. Part of what this means is to "take every thought captive to obey Christ" (2 Cor. 10:5). What is at the core of your heart, God's will or your will?

Have you ever had one of those frantic days, when you are trying to get a ton of things crossed off your "to do" list, but nothing seems to be easy and everything you do is a struggle? I believe that, from time to time, everyone has one of those days. Parents, have you ever yelled at your kids for something that you typically would have ignored, but due to the frustrations of your day you unleashed the pent-up anger upon them? Managers and supervisors, have you done the same to your employees, even though your stress had nothing to do with them? You're not alone. When we do, our temptation is to be of this world, and we get so angry we respond to someone in an ungodly way. Some of us get depressed, go to bed, and try to forget about it. These types of days are when it's most important for us to focus on God's will over *all*, because it is in these moments that our true character is displayed. Instead of throwing in the towel, we are called to rely upon God's supernatural peace to dominate in our lives and rule over *all*.

The apostle Paul wrote in Colossians 3:15, "Let the peace of Christ rule in your hearts, since as members of one body you were called to peace. And be thankful." In the Greek language "rule" comes from the verb *brabeuō*, which was used to describe the action performed by the umpire or referee who moderated and judged the athletic competitions in ancient times.[72] Let the peace of God, in effect, *umpire* or *referee* your hearts, minds, and emotions. When we chose not to let God rule in our lives in this way, we will undoubtedly exhibit the ways of this world, where we are left with anxiety, anger, bitterness, fear, insecurity, doubt, and a whole list of other emotions that will take control. When these sinful emotions rule in our minds, they allow us to become out of control in both our hearts and our actions, disrupting our fellowship with God. When that happens His will no longer reigns in our souls, and often the one destructive emotion that becomes king is bitterness.

Bitterness

When we are offended or disappointed by others' behavior and allow the hurt to germinate in our heart, bitterness and resentment, both of which are sinful and self-defeating, will begin to take root. Bitterness is an immobile form of suppressed anger and resentment, characterized by an unforgiving spirit that is generally negative and critical. Bitterness is created by a constant hurt from a past memory. As our earthly mind holds on to the hurt, the bitterness takes a grip and holds on to us. Let's take a quick inventory and ask ourselves a series of questions to see if we have become a "bitter party of one."

- Is there anyone in your life whom you need to forgive?
- Does anyone's face pop up in your mind when you think of forgiveness?
- When you think of someone who has wronged you, do you get nervous, anxious, or upset?
- Does your heart start to beat faster and your muscles tense up when you think of that person?

- Do you dread attending a function, knowing that someone in particular is going to be present?

If you can relate to any of these questions and answered yes to any of them, then bitterness has sprouted and grown up in your spirit, you need God to reign in your heart, and you need to forgive. We who believe in and belong to Jesus Christ are urged not to allow bitterness to grow among ourselves; we do well to be on the alert when we notice this parasitic emotion taking root in our life or in another person's life. The book of Hebrews issues the warning: "See to it that no one fails to obtain the grace of God; that no 'root of bitterness' springs up and causes trouble, and by it many become defiled" (Heb. 12:15). When bitterness rules in our spirit, it pours out of our pores like a bitter perfume or cologne, and everyone can smell it. I am not saying that a period of time where you separate yourself from the other party may not be beneficial. Oftentimes I believe it is, as the delay allows you time to process. However, if you take too long to deal with the issue and don't allow God to intervene, you can develop a hardened heart.

Forgiveness

Bitterness is perhaps the least healthful emotion we can have, because it disrupts and can destroy our peace of mind, the very peace we are to have with God as the referee of our emotions. This lack of peace is caused because our hardened hearts have created disorder and division within us, alienating us from a life with God. In the Lord's Prayer Jesus asks God to "forgive us our sins, as we have forgiven those who sin against us" (Matt. 6:12 NLT). Forgiveness is so important that in the next sentence Jesus added, "For if you forgive other people when they sin against you, your heavenly Father will also forgive you. But if you do not forgive others their sins, your Father will not forgive your sins" (Matt. 6:14–15). These are harsh words of reality that may be tough to digest, but they are words of truth from God.

People who are bitter have a tendency to remember the tiniest detail as they take inventory of all the wrongs that someone has done in their life. Whenever forgiveness is brought up, they defend their position, asking, "Do you have any idea what I went through? Are you kidding me? You want me to forgive *them*? No way! They don't deserve my forgiveness!" Bitter people constantly defend their grudges. They feel that they have been hurt too deeply and too often and that this exempts them from the need to forgive others, causing them to feel justified in their bitterness. Their hearts are sometimes so full of resentment that they lose the capacity to love and to hear God's message in others.

I agree that forgiveness is challenging. Our faith in Jesus Christ is challenging in and of itself, because such loyalty and allegiance to God calls for us to die to ourselves daily, while everything in this world says to live for ourselves. It is important to remember that forgiveness is not exclusively for the person who did us wrong. Forgiveness is about demonstrating our love for God and allowing His will to be more important to us than our own will. It is in doing God's will that we live in freedom.

We are not alone in the challenge of forgiveness. It would have been much easier for Jesus not to forgive the sinners of the world, but that very thing is exactly what He was called to do. Jesus suffered anguish in the garden at Gethsemane (Mark 14:32–42; Luke 22:39–44). Luke, a physician, tells us in his Gospel that drops of blood literally fell from Jesus' body. In medical terminology this process is called hematidrosis.[73] This process may occur when someone is suffering from extreme levels of stress, such as when facing their own death.[74] This was indeed a crisis for Jesus. Jesus had always obeyed God, His Father, and wanted to continue doing so. Now this meant that He would bear the cross and suffer great pain, humiliation, and an excruciating separation from God, His Father, in the process of dying for our sins. This separation, He knew, would be a far greater difficulty than any of the pain and humiliation He was to endure. Jesus prayed, "My Father! If it is possible, let this cup of suffering be taken away from me. Yet I want your will to be done, not mine" (Matt. 26:39 NLT).

Jesus did not want to suffer the separation from His Father, but He was focused on God's will and not His own. This is what enabled Him, even while hanging on the cross in agony, to pray for His enemies, "Father, forgive them, for they don't know what they are doing" (Luke 23:34). In doing so, He set the ultimate example of forgiveness and love for all generations. When we forgive just as Christ forgave us, it allows us to demonstrate the true love of the gospel and tears down roadblocks that hinder a life of love, joy, and peace with God.

Negative Emotions and Stress on the Body

Bitterness makes everyday life miserable, and whether we know it or not, it can tear down our physical bodies too.[75] Bitterness is an oppressive and destructive emotion that fosters resentment, anger, hate, and other negative emotions, which when not dealt with may lead to violence.[76] These types of emotions allow the enemy to dwell in your life, but God tells us to stand firm in our anger with this command: "In your anger do not sin: Do not let the sun go down while you are still angry, and do not give the devil a foothold" (Eph. 4:26–27 NIV). Remember, if these emotions rule in your life, the enemy has more opportunities to weasel into it.

Bitterness and lack of forgiveness lead to the release of a constant flood of stress hormones that causes the same physical and chemical changes in the body that occur in a speeding person who spies a police officer. Robert Sapolsky said in his book *Why Zebras Don't Get Ulcers*, "We have come to recognize the vastly complex intertwining of our biology and our emotions, the endless ways in which our personalities, feelings, and thoughts both reflect and influence the events in our bodies." He goes on to say that "stress can make us sick."[77]

Chronic stress levels associated with this type of recurrent anger, when left unmanaged, can eventually cause damage to many different systems of the body. Some of the short- and long-term health problems that have been linked to unmanaged anger include:

- Heart attack
- High blood pressure
- Stroke
- Suppressed immune system
- Headache
- Digestion problems
- Insomnia
- Increased anxiety

- Depression
- Skin problems[78]

It is important to note that these health problems are not the cause of disease; they are symptoms of the body's adaptive response to the emotional stress. When we lose control of these adaptive responses, it will impede our ability to live and work optimally for our Lord and Savior, letting the enemy gain influence in our lives. Perhaps we have never really considered the spiritual and ethical dimensions of behaviors that positively or negatively affect our health and sense of well-being, not to mention the potential loss of a full measure of health with which to serve and glorify God in the home, in the church, and in the workplace. We're talking about preventable symptoms here, not chronic illness due to circumstances beyond our control, environmental factors, or problems in our genes.

If you have high blood pressure due to the emotional stress in your life, would taking a high blood pressure pill fix the cause of the high blood pressure? No. You may bring the blood pressure down with the pill, but it does not *fix* the cause. If you become depressed, does taking a "happy pill" or any other psychotropic drug fix the cause? No. In the cases above, when the drug wears off, your blood pressure will go back up and you will become depressed again. If the check engine light comes on in your car, would you cover the light up with a piece of electrical tape so you couldn't see it and assume the problem is fixed? No, that would be absurd. However, this is what we are doing with most of the medications we take to deal with our lack of forgiveness and emotional stressors in our life, while never addressing the true, underlying cause.

Jesus Christ Sets Us As Free As Free Can Be

We who believe are chosen to walk in a life of freedom. As sinners we are slaves to sin, but Jesus said, "If the Son sets you free, you are truly free" (John 8:36). As human beings, and specifically as followers of Jesus Christ, we need to beware of three enemies in life ever seek to re-enslave us: the world (people and systems that oppose Christ), the flesh (corruption that remains in our nature), and the devil (Satan, the enemy of God). Let's see what happens when we break free from the worldly control on our mind and rely upon God.

Proverbs 3:7–8 says, "Don't be impressed with your own wisdom. Instead, fear the LORD and turn away from evil. Then you will have healing for your body and strength for your bones." Our own wisdom is from the world, but when we have reverence or awesome respect for the Lord and let His will reign supreme in our life, we will be filled with the Holy Spirit. This clears the way for God to heal us from our bitterness and other negative attitudes and emotions that cause us to be unwell. Just as darkness is the absence of light, so sickness is the absence of health and evil is the absence of God.

When God is allowed to reign in our hearts, we can have the peace of God, have healing for our whole body and soul, and relief from the evils of bitterness. God says, "A cheerful heart is good medicine, but a crushed spirit dries up the bones" (Prov. 17:22) and "A peaceful heart leads to a healthy body; jealousy is like cancer in the bones" (Prov. 14:30). Research today says much the same: "Improving one's outlook on life and engendering an optimistic attitude may help to reduce the risk of cardiovascular death."[79] Likewise the *Journal of the National Cancer Institute* says, "The people with cancer who deal with their emotions directly have the best outcomes."[80] Did you hear that? Be joyous in the Lord; have laughter in your life. Research shows that laughter has many healing effects, such as regulation of blood sugar and the immune system.[81] This is good news from ancient times!

We can see that the negative emotions in our life, influenced by this world, can have detrimental effects upon our health. On the other hand, having reverence for God and His will in our life can allow us to break free from the chains and bondage of bitterness and other sins, as we learn to forgive others as Christ forgave us, thus loosening the world's death grip and influence on us. This allows for God's sovereignty to reign in our life, giving us peace of mind and health to our whole body. A principle that articulates this exchange is found in Galatians 5:1, where the apostle Paul says, "It is for freedom that Christ has set us free. Stand firm, then, and do not let yourselves be burdened again by a yoke of slavery" (NIV). And elsewhere we read, "Now the Lord is the Spirit, and where the Spirit of the Lord is, there is freedom" (2 Cor. 3:17).

How do we move from being held captive to this world and the allure of our culture and its values to being free in the mind and instead let God's will and peace rule our life? Proverbs 4:20–22 says, "My son, pay attention to what I say; turn your ear to my words. Do not let them out of your sight, keep them within your heart; for they are life to those who find them and health to one's whole body. Above all else, guard your heart, for everything you do flows from it." In these verses God is telling us to protect our heart, where His Spirit dwells with our spirit, by listening to His words. If we do this, it will bring us "life to the fullest." For the believer in Jesus, this is the obedience that comes from faith and is prompted by love (Rom. 1:5; 1 Thess. 1:3).

In the world we live in, we need to be prepared not only to protect our heart but also to prepare ourselves for battle. The enemy is unrelenting in his plots to steal, kill, and destroy us (John 10:10). To prepare for battle we are called to suit up in the armor of God. The Bible says,

> Finally, be strong in the Lord and in his mighty power. Put on the full armor of God, so that you can take your stand against the devil's schemes. For our struggle is not against flesh and blood, but against the rulers, against the authorities, against the powers of this dark world and against the spiritual forces of evil in the heavenly realms. Therefore put on the full armor of God, so that when the day of evil comes, you may be able to stand your ground, and after you have done everything, to stand. Stand firm then, with the belt of truth buckled around your waist, with the breastplate of righteousness in place, and with your feet fitted with the readiness that comes from the gospel of peace. In addition to all this, take up the shield of faith, with which you can extinguish all the flaming arrows of the evil one. Take the helmet of salvation and the sword of the Spirit, which is the word of

God. And pray in the Spirit on all occasions with all kinds of prayers and requests. With this in mind, be alert and always keep on praying for all the saints. (Eph. 6:10–18 NIV)

The Best Defense Is a Good Offense

Imagine walking in the wilderness and coming across a snake. The snake takes the position to attack and you are not able to run away. You have to choose if you are going to defend yourself and prepare for battle or let the snake have its way with you. Now imagine you having a gun. Most of us would most certainly feel more empowered having a gun as a weapon to use for this battle. However, the mere fact of having a gun is futile if you do not know how to use it, and just having the gun in your pocket will not provide protection. Pulling the gun out and pointing it at the snake will not scare it away. However, pointing the gun directly at the snake and pulling the trigger will stop it dead in its approach to attack you. God gives us the weapon to stop the enemy dead in its tracks.

In Ephesians 6:17 we read that our weapon is "the sword of the Spirit, which is the word of God." The sword is our only offensive weapon to be used for the battle with the enemy. All other pieces of the armor of God are there to help us stand steady and firm against him. The Greek word for sword is *machaira*, meaning a relatively short sword or dagger that is used for cutting and stabbing, as distinguished from a large, broad sword.[82] Think of when a knife would be most effective for battle. Would it be better for fighting at a distance or for up-close fighting? You have to be up close, in face-to-face battle, for it to have the most effect. The weapon God gives us to use is perfect, as the enemy is in our face every second of the day, tempting us in this fallen culture in which we live.

We have to be prepared, with our sword in hand and ready to go to battle. However, if we do not believe the battle is of the spiritual realm we will not use the sword of the Spirit. Instead, we will turn to manmade methods of dealing and coping with our battles. It is written in James 1:20, "for man's anger does not bring about the righteous life that God desires." This means that wrath in the mind of man will not have any tendency to make him righteous in the ways of God. The weapon the Spirit wants us to use is the Word of God. When we choose to use a human method, we lose the support from God in the battle because we then are choosing to deal with a spiritual issue with the ways of this world and without using divinely empowered weaponry. In 2 Corinthians 10:4, the apostle Paul says, "We use God's mighty weapons, not worldly weapons, to knock down the strongholds of human reasoning and to destroy false arguments." It is evident that bitterness, from lack of forgiveness, is a spiritual battle that needs God's intervention. We first have to believe that in reality the battle is spiritual and then we have to let the will of God, written in the Word of God and empowered by the Spirit of God, reign in our hearts before we go to battle. Going to battle with any other weapon will lead only to more destruction upon one's self.

The Word of God

As we go into battle we must first understand how to use the mighty weapon God has given us, the Word of God. I would like to briefly describe three Greek words are used in the Bible for the "Word" of God: *graphē*, *logos*, and *rhēma*. While we should acknowledge that each of these words has its own range of meaning and that the circles of their meanings overlap to some extent, the focus here is on some basic distinctions between these terms, as they are used within their contexts.

The first term used in the original Greek is *graphē*. This word refers to the "writings" or "Scriptures" that together are what we call the Bible, which is the written Word of God. The apostle Paul mentioned this term in a letter to a young pastor named Timothy: "All Scripture [*graphē*] is God-breathed and is useful for teaching, rebuking, correcting and training in righteousness, so that the man of God may be thoroughly equipped for every good work" (2 Tim. 3:16–17). Reading the Bible as "*graphē*" is like reading a novel. Anyone, saved or not, can read and understand the Bible from its historical perspective and may ponder the characters and settings. However, just reading the Bible or carrying it around does not provide us any protection from the enemy, just as carrying a gun in our pocket does not provide protection from a venomous snake if the weapon remains concealed and not used.

The second term is *logos*, which refers to the "word" or message we obtain from the written Word of God. Jesus said to His Father in prayer, "Your word [*logos*] is truth" (John 17:17). As followers of Jesus, when we read the Bible, God's

Spirit convinces us of the truth and then convicts us about how to go live it out. The meaning, the message, or the principle of Scripture that the Holy Spirit gives us guides and teaches us in the way of truth, in order to live a godly life. *Logos* affects not only what we do but also how we think. If we were to pull out the gun and point it at another person, the meaning of that action would be clear: *Back off and leave me alone!* But to a snake (or to our enemy, Satan), pulling out a gun as no meaning since the snake is not deterred by the mere sight of a firearm and would continue its attack.

Another verse of Scripture that explains how the *logos* of God's truth works in our lives is Hebrews 4:12: "For the word [*logos*] of God is living and active. Sharper than any double-edged sword, it penetrates even to dividing soul and spirit, joints and marrow; it judges the thoughts and attitudes of the heart." This verse provides us with so much information. First, the term used for "word" here (*logos*) means that God's message is alive, that it has energy. The first law of thermodynamics says, "Energy never dies, it only changes form." Applied spiritually, we could say that God's people need to let the message that is active and alive in the written Word of God (*logos*) change form and be our sword that is sharper than any sword of this world. When we take up and grasp God's Word as our weapon to fight the enemy, God's truth will internally slice and dice our transgressions and sinful nature, which are of this world, out of the way of God's Spirit, allowing Him to break through the barrier we have created as He penetrates our lives with His will. It is at this point that we are carved more and more into the image of Christ as His

Spirit reigns in our hearts, thus controlling our minds and thereby affecting our physical bodies on all levels.

The third Greek term used in the Bible for "word" is *rhēma*. *This word refers to* an utterance, to something declared, or any sound produced by the voice and having definite meaning. When God says in Ephesians 6:17 "Take . . . the sword of the Spirit, which is the word [*rhēma*] of God," He's saying something different from *graphē* or *logos*. *Rhēma* refers to what happens in a battle when the enemy, the snake, is in our face—we are to utter or speak out loud God's Word. *Rhēma* is the weapon the Holy Spirit uses. This is comparable to pulling out a concealed gun, pointing it directly at the snake, and pulling the trigger—bang! The snake is dead. This action is what provides us the protection we need from the enemy.

Let's not be stuck in *graphē*, where we read the Bible but don't absorb His *logos*. Simply reading and carrying a Bible does not provide protection any more than carrying a rabbit's foot or wearing a cross around your neck. We need to move beyond just being inspired or uplifted by God's message (*logos*) on Sundays. We need *rhēma*, where we allow God's *logos* to penetrate deep into our hearts as we speak it out and thus live it in our daily battles, allowing for God's victory to occur in our life.

Dr. Tony Evans nicely summarizes how these three words relate to each other: "In order to be successful in our spiritual struggle, we need to open up and read the Word of God or Scriptures (*graphē*) so that we can understand and be convicted by the meaning (*logos*), directly applying that Word (*rhēma*) to the spiritual struggles (trials and temptations) that we are facing in our everyday lives."[83] This is exactly what Jesus did when he was tempted in the wilderness by the devil: "Jesus answered, 'It is written: "Man does not live on bread alone, but on every word [*rhēma*] that comes from the mouth of God"'" (Matt. 4:4). Likewise, we read in James 4:7, "Submit yourselves, then, to God. Resist the devil, and he will flee from you." If we *do not* do this, we will become a casualty of spiritual warfare, and our attempts to serve the Lord will be hindered, not only spiritually but also physically. Pursuing health and wellness means much more than just surviving—it means thriving and winning spiritual battles.

Action Steps

1. Starting with a clear conscience, repent to God and ask for forgiveness. Be sure to forgive others; otherwise God will not forgive you.
2. Embrace God's Word; hold it close to your heart and do what it says.
3. Recognize that in reality the battle is spiritual.
4. Speak God's Word out loud when you are engaged in a battle, as this is the only offensive weapon we have to achieve victory against the devil's schemes. Speak His Word with authority and allow it to bring you peace.

CHAPTER 7

Emptiness on a Full Stomach

*"The devil has put a penalty on all things we enjoy in life.
Either we suffer in health or we suffer in soul or we get fat."*
Albert Einstein

*"So whether you eat or drink or whatever you do,
do it all for the glory of God."*
1 Corinthians 10:31

Have you ever seen a movie where a girl gets dumped by her boyfriend and in the very next scene you see her going to the freezer to grab a gallon of ice cream? Sure, this is Hollywood, but it's not far from reality. Let me give you an example of a real life situation involving my wife and comfort food.

Food for the Hurting

After my wife and I got married, we knew we wanted to start a family right away—it was rare to see us in public without our nieces and nephews. You can imagine our disappointment when it took over a year to get pregnant.

After finally becoming pregnant, we lost our baby during the second trimester. This was incredibly painful, both physically and emotionally, for my wife. Sparing all the details, I can tell you that the day we lost our baby began one horrifically painful event after another. In hope of to becoming pregnant again and to prepare my wife's body for a healthy pregnancy, we sought out a doctor who would guide us in creating within my wife's body a hospitable environment for a baby to grow. This was evidently part of the problem. This doctor's advice involved changing the way my wife ate and how she exercised. The one thing the doctor emphasized was the fact that her body was not ready to be pregnant, and thus he told us that whatever we do, don't get pregnant right away.

However, only a few short months later, way before her body was ready, we found ourselves pregnant again. Early into this pregnancy my wife again started to show signs that something was wrong. Having been through this same physical and emotional trauma a few months prior, I was prepared to call the doctor, take her to the hospital, and do anything that she asked, but in that moment what she asked for took me by surprise. My wife looked at me, gripped my arm while clearly in pain, and said, "Get me a cheeseburger and fries *now!*"

Please keep in mind that this is after my wife had been working hard at getting healthy by eating impeccably and exercising daily. This was also a period of time where we were not grounded in our faith. Thus, when she started showing signs of miscarriage again, she was crushed. With this turn of events she felt that all her efforts were pointless and she felt no sense of hope. Do I think it was wrong that my wife wanted to eat a cheeseburger and fries? No. What was wrong was the timing. In hindsight, this was an obvious example of her using food to fill a void and cover up her physical and emotional pain. Can food really cover-up cover up pain and provide us with comfort?

Stick with me through another story, and I will show you that food can absolutely mask our pain and provide "comfort." When our first son was born I was so happy and joyous. However, I also watched anyone and everyone who came near my son like a hawk. Jesus said that no one gets to the Father except through Him; well, I was saying no one gets to my son except through me. In the hospital nobody was allowed to leave the room with him unless I went along. The nurse came in to take him for his circumcision, so of course I followed. In the course of the procedure I discovered something very interesting. They put on a rubber glove, dipped it in sugar water, and then stuck it in his mouth before starting the procedure. I had forgotten why they did that, so I asked. The nurse said, "Because it decreases the pain sensation in the body."

The Painkilling Power of Sugar

This reminded me of a fascinating book called *Potatoes Not Prozac* by Kathleen DesMaisons.[84] In this book the author talks about research done in the mid 1980s by Dr. Elliott Blass,[85] who conducted some interesting studies on the use of sugar as a safe analgesic (pain relief) for babies. Initially, Dr. Blass wondered how long mice can stand the heat of a hot plate without any painkillers. He found that the mice would stand an average of ten seconds before lifting their paws off the hot plate. Then he gave the mice a solution of 11.5 percent sugar and repeated the experiment. This time it took twice as long before the mice would lift their feet from the hot plate—twenty seconds. This suggested that the sugar was acting like a painkiller.

Dr. Blass then hypothesized that the sugar was acting like an opioid, causing a release of the natural painkiller, beta-endorphin. To test his hypothesis Dr. Blass used the drug Naltrexone, known to block the painkilling effect of opioid drugs, such as heroin and morphine. This time in the experiment, before giving the mice the sugar drink, Dr. Blass gave the mice a dose of Naltrexone. Then he tested their reaction time to the heat from the hot plate. This time the mice lifted their feet up in eight seconds. This confirmed that sugar affects the brain in the same way opioid drugs do, by stimulating the release of beta-endorphins.

In the same year of this experiment Dr. Blass reported results from his experiments on the effects of sugar on emotional pain. In the experiment he took away eight baby mice from their mother and measured how many times they cried in a six-minute period, since they did not normally cry while in the presence of their mother. Initially, when taken away, the baby mice cried three hundred times in the six-minute period. However, when they were given the sugar solution they cried only seventy-five times in the same time period. Next, Dr. Blass gave them the Naltrexone before the sugar solution and the baby mice cried as often as those who had not received the sugar (some three hundred times). This confirmed that the sugar was not only blocking the physical pain but also emotional pain.

Given this summary of Dr. Blass's research, it is no wonder that the majority of "comfort food" that people consume while "stress eating" is laden with high levels of carbohydrates and simple sugars. Essentially, when we are overwhelmed with stress, oftentimes due to the lack of God's will being priority in our life, we turn toward comfort food and try to eat away our physical and emotional pain. However, it is to God that we should be turning in times of stress. In the Garden of Gethsemane, we do not read that Jesus was gorging Himself with breads and wines to seek comfort. We read that He began to pray to His Father in heaven (see Matt. 26:35–45).

Comfort Food As a Quick Fix

We live in a world full of stress, and how do we handle it? Do we do as Jesus did and immediately start praying? Let's take inventory of our habits for a moment. What is our typical reaction when we have a stressful day, where we are experiencing physical or emotional pain? What is typically the first thing we turn to? Is it an alcoholic drink, a sugary sweet, a fried fatty food, a cigarette, an over-the-counter medication? Research shows that these things can temporarily make us feel better since ingesting them can change our body chemistry, but eating such things does not make us healthy physically, chemically, emotionally, or spiritually.

Fallen human nature is such that we tend to gravitate toward things that provide instant gratification and quick fixes, especially in today's society. This behavior is not detrimental when done occasionally, but it becomes a problem when we behave like Pavlov's dogs.[86] Pavlov conducted a classical experiment revealing the behavior of a conditioned response. Pavlov would present dogs with a ringing bell that was followed by food. The food would create an unconditioned response of salivation, as it is an inherent response in preparation for food digestion. After repeated pairings of the bell and food, the food was removed and the bell alone now elicited salivation, turning an inherent unconditioned response into a conditioned response. Our culture has created a society where we routinely turn toward these quick fixes for instant relief, as a conditioned response, the moment we encounter a stress. As we allow these things to be our "first-aid cabinet," so to speak, the dominoes begin to fall. It has been proven in research that satisfaction cannot be stored in the memory and must be continually renewed.[87] This behavior of instant gratification quickly becomes habitual as it leads to imbalances that create destruction of God's temple. The comfort that is achieved will soon cease to satisfy, allowing us to crave more.

Thus, as we encounter one stress and relieve it temporarily through external means such as food or drugs, the next time the body encounters the stress it will not have a memory of satisfaction. This will lead to the need for more of the substance of choice to get the desired effect. This is how addictions are created and why, in general, we are always looking for something bigger and better in this world of overindulgence.

"Keeping up with the Joneses" is prevalent in our culture. People typically want a nicer car, bigger house, more money, and so on. Same thing with drugs and alcohol. Addicts are always looking for a bigger and better high or buzz, respectively.

A journal article in *Scientific American* titled "Carbohydrates and Depression" reported that "[w]hen carbohydrate cravers were asked why they succumb to foods they know will exacerbate their obesity, their explanation sounded much like the one provided by SAD [seasonal affective disorder] sufferers. It almost never had to do with hunger or with the taste of the food; instead, most said they eat to combat tension, anxiety, or mental fatigue. After eating, the majority reported feeling calm and clearheaded."[88] Neuroscientist and pharmacologist Candace Pert states in her book *Molecules of Emotion*, "I consider sugar to be a drug, a highly purified plant product that can become addictive." She goes on to say, "Relying on an artificial form of glucose—sugar—to give us a quick pick-me-up is analogous to, if not as dangerous as shooting heroin."[89] According to another research study, *refined sugar is far more addictive than cocaine*, which is one of the most addictive and harmful substances currently known. The researchers stated, "Our findings clearly demonstrate that intense sweetness can surpass cocaine reward, even in drug-sensitized and addicted individuals."[90]

Marketing Food to the Masses

Researchers have established that there is a biochemical reaction that occurs in the brain with regard to food and drugs, which can create a chemical dependency in times of stress. But make no mistake about it: the food industry and many other industries absolutely know that we use food and other substances to self-medicate, and in order to feed on our emotions they market to us in a way that reinforces this behavior, for their financial gain. Let me provide a few examples:

1. A particular potato chip manufacturer uses to tagline "Happiness is simple."

2. Another potato chip manufacturer says, "Happiness in a Bag."

3. A maker of cutlery has "A slice of happiness" on a pie spatula, "A scoop full of comfort" on a spoon, and "A dab of decadence" on a spreading knife.

These are just a few of the many ads that inundate us daily. This type of marketing is not only geared toward adults; it is also targeted to our children. Think of the term "Happy Meal." This is the most obvious display of marketing sending the message of "comfort food" to children. There's even a Happy Meal website with games, videos, toys, and activities! This type of marketing is significantly affecting the younger generation of today. A study in the *Journal of Pediatrics* concluded that TV ads trump parents when it comes to the food choices young children make.[91] Do not misinterpret this and say "Well, as a parent I make no difference." That's not necessarily true. Media influence and peer dependence are strong factors. But the potential to make a lasting generational impact is enormous, especially for our children, as we lead them in all areas of life by example, including food choices and eating habits.

I mentioned in an earlier chapter that we no longer refer to adult onset diabetes because children are now being diagnosed with this condition, as well as with heart disease, which are both lifestyle diseases. This occurs because a diet depleted in nutrients and laden with manmade chemicals creates an inflammatory response in the body. Inflammation is a natural process that the body uses in response to injury and to fight infections. The textbook *Robbins Pathologic Basis of Disease* states, "Even in the era of burgeoning global affluence, nutritional imbalances continue to be major causes of cell injury."[92] In today's culture, where we eat food with processed chemicals made by man that is deficient in the nutrients needed to sustain optimal function, we create cellular injury continuously. This dietary imbalance can cause a chronic, low-grade, systemic state of inflammation. Chronic systemic inflammation has been linked to every major degenerative disease in industrialized nations. From cardiovascular disease and cancer to osteoporosis and arthritis, inflammation has been called "the engine" that drives the degenerative lifestyle diseases of today, diabetes included.

If we do not stand firm as leaders for the generation coming up behind us and demonstrate in our daily lives and behaviors the boundaries and principles that are laid out for us in the Bible, they will mimic how we eat and live. As Christians, we need to live a life that is congruent with the biblical principles we claim to hold dear to our heart, or we will continuously edge God's will out of our life. This can have consequences that can last an eternity, as our current generational trends reveal the behavior of our youth today as "monkey see, monkey do." If we are not leading as Christ would lead, we may be encouraging a life separated from God in those who follow us. We must take a moment for a gut check and ask ourselves, "How well are we leading?"

Church Potlucks, Picnics, and . . . Sinful Eating?

We should not replace God with eating or drinking to sustain us through hardship. When we turn first to these things in times of stress, we begin to edge out God in our lives. The purpose of eating and drinking is to sustain our bodies and in some situations to celebrate. A snapshot of the early church in Jerusalem looked like this: "Every day they continued to meet together in the temple courts. They broke bread in their homes and ate together with glad and sincere hearts, praising God and enjoying the favor of all the people. And the Lord added to their number daily those who were being saved" (Acts 2:46–47). Feasts in the Old Testament and the "potlucks" of the early church serve to indicate that celebration is a legitimate reason for eating and drinking. They did it while praising the Lord, but in today's society we need to be cautious, as we have a tendency instead to "praise the lard." We are flooded with opportunities to eat high calorie, nutrient deficient foods laden with sugar; we need to be mindful and not overindulge.

Researcher Matthew Feinstein from Northwestern University Feinberg School of Medicine stated the following; "Our main finding was that people with a high frequency of religious participation in young adulthood were 50 percent more likely to become obese by middle age than those with no religious participation in young adulthood." He added, "We didn't look specifically at the potluck factor, but anecdotally, we know that oftentimes at these religious gatherings people will eat traditional comfort foods which are often high in fat and calories and salt."[93] By quoting this research I am not saying that we shouldn't attend church functions if we want to maintain a healthy weight. I am saying we should be more diligent in our daily food intake to offset the times we celebrate with less than nutritious food. On the other hand, maybe we should be eating daily and celebrating with the foods God provides for us to enjoy that best contribute to optimizing our overall health spiritually, physically, chemically, and emotionally.

There is no doubt that the "comfort foods" in which people are overindulging are contributing to the leading causes of death in America. Are you making the connections here? Remember, all parts of the body are interconnected, and they all depend upon each other for proper function. In order for the cells of our body to function properly together, they must also have the correct fuel. The fuel that our body depends upon in proper balance includes vitamins, minerals, water, protein, fats, and carbohydrates. When we are deficient in or in excess of any of these nutrients, it causes the body to compensate, which oftentimes leads to dysfunction and unfavorable symptoms. And it is all these years of dysfunction that further the symptoms of "dis-ease" to disease.[94]

The apostle Paul gave instruction to Christians that provided a principle to guide them in the exercise of their freedom, an instruction that we can apply to what we eat and why we're eating it: "'Everything is permissible for me'—but not everything is beneficial. 'Everything is permissible for me'—but I will not be mastered by anything. . . . [and] not everything is constructive" (1 Cor. 6:12; 10:23). The litmus test for addiction that I offered earlier is the question "Does it control you or do you control it?"

Now let me clear the air: It is not a sin to go out and have a burger and fries, pie, cake, or any other food substance, for that matter. As the Bible says, "Can't you see that the food you put into your body cannot defile you" (Mark 7:18 NLT). It becomes a sin, however, when you use food as a substitute for God. The Bible says, "You shall have no other gods before me" (Exod. 3:20). Idolatry, the worshiping of anything other than God, is clearly a sin. Paul in Philippians 3:18–19 criticizes self-indulgent Christians for not living up to Christ's model of self-sacrifice and servanthood: "For, as I have often told you before and now tell you again even with tears, many live as enemies of the cross of Christ. Their destiny is destruction, their god is their stomach, and their glory is in their shame. Their mind is set on earthly things."

This verse says that our stomachs can become our god. Physical appetites are an analogy of our ability to control ourselves in the moral dimensions of life, such as avoiding lust and not coveting. Consider this definition of an idol from theologian and professor James M. Grier: "An idol represents the power of a culture to get the citizens of that culture to live by a particular lifestyle."[95] Fast food, anyone? Does it matter to God what food we eat, how much we eat, and why we eat what we choose to eat? Eating can clearly be very sinful if we let our appetites rule us. Additionally, if our minds are set on earthly things, such as the vanity of making our bodies look a certain way (e.g., super thin), a lack of eating can become sinful. Whether in excess or in absence, the eating or not eating of food can be sinful if done for reasons that are not honoring to God.

Gluttony seems to be a sin that Christians like to ignore. A glutton can be defined as "a person with a remarkably great desire or capacity for something."[96] We are often quick to label smoking, drinking, and internet pornography as sins, but for some reason gluttony of food is accepted or at least tolerated. Many of the arguments used against smoking and drinking, such as health problems and addiction, apply equally to unhealthy eating habits. Many believers would not even consider having a glass of wine or smoking a cigarette but have no qualms about gorging themselves on "comfort food" in times of stress. This should not be!

Proverbs 23:20–21 warns us, "Do not join those who drink too much wine or gorge themselves on meat, for drunkards and gluttons become poor, and drowsiness clothes them in rags." Proverbs 28:7 declares, "He who keeps the law is a discerning son, but a companion of gluttons disgraces his father." Proverbs 23:2 says, "Put a knife to your throat if you are given to gluttony." We're not to let our appetites control us, but rather we are to control our appetites. We should eat to live, not live to eat. The ability to say no to anything in excess—self-control—is one of the fruits of the Spirit common to all believers (Gal. 5:22). We are much happier if God rules our lives and if our minds are set on eternal things, as God commands. God has blessed us by filling the earth with foods that are delicious, nutritious, and even pleasurable to eat. We should honor God's creation by enjoying these foods and by eating them in appropriate quantities, while controlling our appetites rather than allowing them to control us.

Avoiding the Diet of America's Cultural Values

Many find it hard to control their appetites, particularly when they are like the frog being slow-cooked to death in the pot of water—they don't recognize that their appetite is controlling them. Others feel they are addicted; therefore they cannot stop their behavior. Some feel they cannot avoid the daily temptations as they are inundated by the media and marketing efforts of our culture.

We are not alone in this predicament; Daniel was taken over nine hundred miles from his home to the land of Babylonia, where he would serve a new king as a slave. In the book of Daniel we read that "the king assigned them [Daniel and his three Hebrew friends] a daily amount of food and wine from the king's table. They were to be trained for three years, and after that they were to enter the king's service" (Dan. 1:5). "But Daniel resolved not to defile himself with the royal food and wine, and he asked the chief official for permission not to defile himself this way" (Dan. 1:8). Daniel pleaded, "Please test your servants for ten days: Give us nothing but vegetables to eat and water to drink. Then compare our appearance with that of the young men who eat the royal food, and treat your servants in accordance with what you see" (Dan. 1:12–13). "At the end of the ten days they looked healthier and better nourished than any of the young men who ate the royal food" (Dan. 1: 15).

It appears that Daniel chose not to partake of the royal food because it was "unclean" and against the Mosaic laws of the Old Testament, not to mention unhealthy. Also, his resolve demonstrated that he had chosen to not become part of the Babylonian culture by eating and drinking as they did. It may be that the meat had been offered to the gods of Babylonia, much as the New Testament describes in the first century (see Acts 15:29; 1 Cor. 8; 10:14–22). Do not think this was easy for Daniel; he had to be intentional in demonstrating his resolve. Daniel was tempted daily, just as we are, as he was plunged into the Babylonian culture. For Daniel to achieve victory over the ungodly culture of Babylonia, he had to have bone deep resolve, as godliness is never accidental. Daniel had to have the integrity to be consistent in all his ways. Integrity can be defined as the quality or condition of being whole or undivided; completeness.[97] You can see in the book of Daniel that he did not live with a divided heart, wavering back and forth between being godly as a Jewish exile and being ungodly as a Babylonian pagan. He was consistent in all his ways to honor God.

Remember that it is our areas of inconsistency that become the bull's-eye for the devil's flaming arrows. We are not going to be perfect; if we were, we would be Jesus. But God does call us to be faithful. The point is that Jesus was hung on a cross for our sins. We don't have to be perfect, but I do believe that by God's grace, through faith, we can and should strive to reach consistency in all aspects of our life. It's a lifelong endeavor. Let's be like Daniel, resisting the endless, crashing waves of temptation that hit us every day, telling us, "Conform to the ways of this world." Instead, let's live intentionally, with integrity.

Dare to Be a Daniel

But how do we become like Daniel in our modern-day Babylonia when many of us feel like Paul as he describes himself in Romans 7:14–23:

> We know that the law is spiritual; but I am unspiritual, sold as a slave to sin. I do not understand what I do. For what I want to do I do not do, but what I hate I do. And if I do what I do not want to do, I agree that the law is good. As it is, it is no longer I myself who do it, but it is sin living in me. For I know that good itself does not dwell in me, that is, in my sinful nature. For I have the desire to do what is good, but I cannot carry it out. For I do not do the good I want to do, but the evil I do not want to do—this I keep on doing. Now if I do what I do not want to do, it is no longer I who do it, but it is sin living in me that does it. So I find this law at work: Although I want to do good, evil is right there with me. For in my inner being I delight in God's law; but I see another law at work in me, waging war against the law of my mind and making me a prisoner of the law of sin at work within me.

Wow, can any of you relate to this? There is a daily battle going on inside of us, and in a very real sense it is our decision that determines who wins: do I live according to what God says in the Word or according to the dictates of my flesh, the remaining corruption and pull of sinful habits that I must put to death even as a Christian. Paul goes on to say, "What a wretched man I am! Who will rescue me from this body that is subject to death?" (Rom. 8:24). Who will rescue him—Dr. Phil,

Dr. Oz, Dr. Bentley, or Oprah? No! He says, "Thanks be to God, who delivers me through Jesus Christ our Lord!" (Rom. 8:25).

We should ask ourselves,

- Why am I eating? What need does this meet? Am I eating to live or living to eat?
- Am I focused and doing the work of God, or am I avoiding important issues in my life?
- Do I eat because of boredom, laziness, idleness, depression, discouragement, self-pity, or feeling overwhelmed?
- Do I not eat because of vanity or for trying to achieve a certain look with my body?
- Do people know me as one who is often eating or not eating?
- Do thoughts of food rule my day?
- Do I turn to food to medicate and distract me from dealing with my problems?
- Am I mastered by my appetite? Is my stomach my God? Do I crave food and show little restraint in the area of eating?
- Do I use food to get me through my day?
- Do I ever fast and pray as a Christian for biblical reasons?

Bottom line is, if we are eating or drinking habitually for the purpose of escaping hardships in life, or our desire for something of this earth is greater than our desire for God in our life, then we are gluttons and are creating a separation from a fully aligned life with God. Essentially, we are spoiling our appetites with things of this earth and losing our hunger for the meat of God's Word. It is written, "So whether you eat or drink, or whatever you do, do it all for the glory of God" (1 Cor. 10:31).

From a nutritional standpoint the dictum "Eat food. Not too much. Mostly plants"[98] may just be the short answer to the perplexing question of what people should eat for optimal health and wellness. I am not insisting that one needs to be a vegan or vegetarian, as the situation after the flood described in Genesis 9:3 makes clear in terms of God's intentions: "Everything that lives and moves will be food for you. Just as I gave you the green plants, I now give you everything." Likewise, we read in 1 Timothy 4:3–5: "[Hypocritical liars whose conscience doesn't work] . . . order [people] to abstain from certain foods, which God created to be received with thanksgiving by those who believe and who know the truth. For everything God created is good, and nothing is to be rejected if it is received with thanksgiving, because it is consecrated by the word of God and prayer."

Note that this passage says "Everything God created is good," not "everything man created is good." The Bible is clear that God, not man, made food. Unfortunately, it is the "manmade" food that most Americans eat, and it leads to the destruction of God's vessels. I believe that it's our duty to God as Christians to be thriving vessels for his good works. Thus, every time we start to eat we must take heed of what is about to enter our body, His vessel. Does it build us up? Or does it break us down? If you need help determining the answer to those two questions, simply ask yourself, *Who "made" this food, man or God?* But in any case, let's become like Daniel and be consistently intentional about honoring God in all our ways, food choices and eating habits included. That's a tall order, "but with God all things are possible" (Matt. 19:26).

CHAPTER 8

Movement

"How often we expect big things from God without preparing for big things from Him."
Beth Moore

"Do not merely listen to the word, and so deceive yourselves. Do what it says."
James 1:22

The benefits of physical movement, such as exercise, are numerous and will be the main focus of this chapter. But even more important is the idea of "movement upon" God's Word, of putting God's truth into practice (Matt. 7:24–27). A key verse that affirms the former and yet places greater value on the latter is 1 Timothy 4:8: "For physical training is of some value, but godliness has value for all things, holding promise for both the present life and the life to come."

Godliness, in simple terms, is being like God. When we think like God thinks, say what God says, and do what God does, we bear a strong family resemblance to Jesus. This is what people noticed about the apostles after the Holy Spirit came and filled them with power and boldness, as Jesus had promised: "When they saw the courage of Peter and John and realized that they were unschooled, ordinary men, they were astonished and they took note that these men had been with Jesus" (Acts 4:13). Of Jesus more than anyone else, the statement was true: "I do nothing on my own but speak just what the Father has taught me" (John 8:28). Jesus moved upon God's Word, *literally*. To the extent that this applies to those of us who follow Jesus today, God wants us to move upon His Word with the obedience of faith. When God by His Spirit prompts us to do something for His glory, do we obey or throw a wet blanket on His fire? We will discover how both forms of "movement" will enhance our mind and our faith and bring health to one's body.

What does it mean to move on God's Word? How do we discern if the subjective experience we feel prompting us is from God, the devil, or ourselves and our emotions? What does God "feel" like? This is a subject of debate among many theologians. I am not a theologian, nor do I claim to be one. However, I do search, research, and study truth. Thus, what I am sharing with you is from my experiences in life and the Word of God.

Spiritual Movement

For the most part, I was not brought up in church and never attended, except for Christmas and Easter. Growing up, I wasn't taught what it means to be a believer in Jesus Christ and to have a personal relationship with Him. However, I will say that I was brought up with a good and clear understanding of right and wrong. Many of my personal convictions were taught to me by family members, teachers, coaches, parents of friends, and my friends. Sometimes it was from a direct representation of how they lived their lives that I formed my convictions. However, I often learned what not to do from many of their negative examples as well.

I was not perfect growing up, nor am I perfect now. Nevertheless, I remember the feeling of uneasiness that was in my life when I was in college. I did not like the person I was becoming, when I was on my own for the first time, as I had started to lower my personal standards and make exceptions to give in to certain temptations in my life. Although it was early on, I felt my lifestyle choices during a certain period of six months were creating a less than fruitful life.

At the same time there was a close friend of mine who had grown up knowing the Lord but who had been on a destructive path for about two years. One day he said, "That's it. I'm going back to church!" For some reason I volunteered to go with him as a support. Wow, I had no idea what I was in for that night. First we pulled up to a building with a neon sign that said "Church," and to avoid judging a book by its cover, I continued with my friend into the church. People were singing, dancing, laughing, hugging, and the like. Next there were people crying and praying on their knees. I remember looking around, saying to myself, *What's wrong with these people?* Next thing I knew, like a flash of lightening, I was watching a movie of all the bad choices I had made in my life and, more recently, of the many exceptions I had made, eroding my integrity, which was slowly fading away. After that I was on my knees, asking Jesus to be my Lord and Savior.

This was the first prompting in my life from the Holy Spirit. After I received Jesus as my Savior, the Holy Spirit took up residence and dwelled within me and began to guide me in my life, if I obeyed God's Word and allowed His will to have the final say in my life. In John 16:13 Jesus says, "But when he, the Spirit of truth, comes, he will guide you into all the truth. He will not speak on his own; he will speak only what he hears, and he will tell you what is yet to come."

For many of us the question still remains, *How do we recognize the prompting from God?* Some authors say, "When you have peace." Others say, "It's a feeling." We need to be careful and not just go with a feeling or a sense of peace. I have met many people who said they "had a feeling" so they did what they felt prompted to do. Unfortunately, in one case of following a "feeling," the individual promptly committed adultery. That's not God's will, because it contradicts His Word (Exod. 20:14; Matt. 5:26–28). God does not prompt us to gratify the flesh. The enemy loves to play games with us, trick us, and tempt us. Thus before we move on a prompting that we feel is of the Holy Spirit, we need to make sure it's biblical and follows Scripture, rightly interpreted in context. God never tells us to do anything that goes against His written Word.

Rare are the apparent contradictions in the story of the Bible, as when God commanded Abraham to sacrifice his son as a burnt offering, the one and only son, Isaac, whom the patriarch loved and through whom God had promised many descendants (Gen. 22). Likewise, the sacrifice and death of God's one and only Son, whom He loved, blows all of our categories—amazing love, at such an incredible price to pay

(John 3:16; Rom. 5:8; 8:32). Such anomalies in the will and providence of God have their purpose in testing our faith or in reasons not revealed to us and that only God knows. But in every other case God guides according to and in keeping with His written Word. This is why it is important to spend time studying the Bible because the better we know what God says, the easier it will be for us to identify His voice. Additionally, you may do what I often do, and that is to seek out counsel from others who are living their lives according to God's Word (Prov. 15:22) and have more knowledge about the Bible than I do. The Bible is the Word of God, and He has laid out very clearly the moral boundaries and direction for living life. If we're seeking guidance from God in health, parenting, marriage, business, finances, or whatever, Scripture can offer us guidance with the help of the Holy Spirit.

Variety Is Often the Spice of Life

Prompting from God may come in many different forms for different people. It could be an unsettling feeling, a peacefulness, or a word or phrase that comes to mind. This kind of thing makes some people, including many Christians, uneasy. It is not for me to judge or say that all the ways of God's wisdom and omniscience can be revealed to us. Even Scripture represents only what God has chosen to reveal to us, but it's always enough. The apostle Peter puts it this way: "His divine power has given us everything that is necessary for life and godliness through our knowledge of him who called us by his own glory and goodness" (2 Peter 1:3; cf. 2 Peter 1:19–21). All I can say is, when you have that "feeling," make sure the act you feel prompted to do is fully aligned with God's Word, and if so, then act on it. Don't second-guess what God tells you to do.

For example, one day I was shopping with my oldest child, who at that time was about two years old. He was buckled securely in the seat of the shopping cart when I stopped and turned away from him to look for an item on the shelf; an unsettling feeling crept over my body, and inexplicable words popped up into my mind, *Turn around!* Without hesitation, I turned with my arm stretched out and hand wide open to find it landing on my son's waistline, where I grabbed the junction of his shirt and pants. Suddenly, gasps from spectators occurred in surround sound, as I had just caught my son midair on his way to the cement floor—head first.

Some people may call this intuition or Jedi reflexes; however, if you have put your faith and trust in Jesus Christ as I have, then you know it is the Holy Spirit. Does the Holy Spirit really lead us in everyday matters such as in the previous story? Yes, He does. No matter how big or small the situation, God leads us. The closer we follow Him and the quicker we are to listen to His promptings, the more we know the Holy Spirit is functioning in our life.

The Spirit and the Word Go Together

Learning to discern God's voice can be a challenging task when we first begin to listen for Him in our daily life, especially when you do not have an in-depth knowledge of His Word. It is not a requirement to be a biblical scholar in order to recognize God's voice. Think about how many ordinary people in the Bible God used, despite their sometimes limited faith, to do amazing things (see Hebrews 11). However, listening to these prompts becomes easier the more we study Scripture and the more we act on them. It is much like exercising a muscle; the more you use it, the stronger and more stable it becomes.

Look at it as spiritual fitness and training. I think back to when we first bought our dog. I had to train the puppy to live according to my rules. It took time for the puppy to recognize my voice and the commands I would give her, but over time she became obedient to my voice and the boundaries I set for her. In the same way, the Bible is the Word of God that teaches us what truth is and helps us realize what is wrong in our lives. When we are actively seeking God's truth, the Bible corrects us when we are wrong and teaches us to do what is right (2 Tim. 3:16).

We can quickly discern if we have heard and acted incorrectly because we will not feel rested in our spirit when we are making wrong choices. We will not have the peace promised to us from God when His will reigns in our lives (Rom. 8:6). On the other hand, if we have heard correctly, we will feel a rising peace and confidence at the action taken. Either way, right or wrong, I can tell you God loves us: "And we know that in all things God works for the good of those who love him, who have been called according to his purpose" (Rom. 8:28). I am not suggesting you make wrong decisions and everything will be fine. I am saying that if you happen to misjudge your prompting, you will have an unsettling feeling within you and this can be the point at which you can repent, confess your mistake, and ask for forgiveness.

Then turn from it and do not do it anymore. True repentance is to turn from a wrong action 180 degrees and do the opposite, right action. This shows that not only have we realized our mistake, but we are repenting and doing the right thing God has called us to do (see, e.g., 2 Cor. 7:10). There are times we are weak, but the Holy Spirit recognizes our weaknesses and prays for us, according to the will of God. Paul writes in Romans 8:26–27, "In the same way, the Spirit helps us in our weakness. We do not know what we ought to pray for, but the Spirit himself intercedes for us through wordless groans. And he who searches our hearts knows the mind of the Spirit, because the Spirit intercedes for God's people in accordance with the will of God."

Following God's will for our lives is often neither fun nor comfortable. We may not always understand the promptings from the Holy Spirit, but it is okay because Jesus was not interested in raising a family of believers who only had faith when they understood everything. We are called to a level of excellence, as we are His sanctuary, and to be set apart from the rest of the world. Most of us are just ordinary people, but were called to have extraordinary lives of faith, with His will at the center of our hearts and our minds. Yet sometimes our faith is small, but that's okay—it's enough for God to work with.

I often hear patients and acquaintances say, "I do not like my job, I do not feel I am serving my purpose in my life, I want to do . . . but I can't because I have good health insurance, or I make great money." I understand that mentality; I have been there myself, but there is nothing more liberating and exciting than to decide to live your life according to God's purpose. Sometimes God asks us to do something that seems irrational to our rational minds. In situations like this, many friends may think and tell you that you are foolish as you follow His command.

I remember the first time I read Genesis 22, which I mentioned earlier, where God told Abraham to sacrifice his only son, Isaac. I thought he was crazy to do it, but Abraham knew the command was from God and not the devil. Thus he obeyed God, and just before he would have sacrificed his son God provided a ram. Due to Abraham's obedience God continued to multiply Abraham's lineage through Isaac (Heb. 11:17–19). I have been in situations where friends and family thought that my actions where insane, and they thought I was making a big mistake, but my promptings were from God, and this next story illustrates it perfectly.

Discerning Unexpected Movement and Holding On for the Ride

On August 2, 2008, a great friend, who was also a brother in Christ and a father of three children, was killed in an automobile accident at the young age of thirty-seven. During that time, like many people do, I spent a lot of time reflecting on my own life and the direction I was heading. As I realized how short life really is, I started praying over and over and over, "God, use me, I want to be your vessel; I want to serve your purpose that you have for me."

While I was out in Colorado with his family and friends, my wife's best friend's father unexpectedly died. Thus when I flew back from Colorado, we immediately left to be with my wife's friend and family. After about four hours, as we left the town where we were visiting, I looked over at my wife and said, "If I ever retire, I can totally live here. I have an overwhelming sense of peace, love, and family here." My wife said, "I had that exact same feeling."

As we were traveling back to pick up our kids from my in-laws' house, my wife's mom called and said, "Plan on staying a while before you head home. We're having a barbecue with all your nieces and nephews." My wife looked at me and said, "How nice would it be to live an hour and a half from our family and have barbecues often?" I immediately replied, "Don't get any ideas. We'll never move, and I'll never sell my practice."

As we continued to drive, I talked with my wife about the amounts of stress I was under, trying to run my new practice, write books, lecture to doctors on the weekends, and personally train doctors in functional medicine during the week. I mentioned to her that I should bring another doctor into my practice; she agreed. A few days later, I called one of my favorite professors and left a message for him to give me a call if he knew of anybody who would fit into my practice; as he knew my faith and the level of knowledge I would expect a doctor to have to come into my practice. He returned my call the following day and said, "I have an entire class graduating tomorrow and there is not one person I can recommend for you. However, if you don't mind waiting till December, I have the perfect guy for you, and he already has your phone number." I replied, "Why does he already have my number?" He responded, "When you called and left a message he was in my office saying that he wanted to move to your town. I told him that he had to call you so you could show him around and help get him started in practice, since you have a lot in common. I will make sure he calls you in the next hour."

The call came an hour later, and we discovered that we did have a lot in common, not only very similar personalities, but his wife, whom he had married four and a half months prior, was a massage therapist and a doctor's assistant. This was interesting because at the time my massage therapist was leaving for graduate school, and my assistant was leaving for a three-month maternity leave. I invited this young doctor to come down and check out the practice, because I had a great associate position available, and it sounded as though we were a perfect fit. I said, "If nothing else you will get some ideas for your own practice." He replied, "Oh, I was looking at buying a practice." I said, "I don't have any plans of selling my practice, but who knows what the future may bring?" So we set a date for him to come down and check out what I had to offer.

Three days later I was in church praying for God to use me for His purpose. I wanted to be His vessel, to live for Him and not myself, especially in light of the recent reinforcements in my situation of the brevity of life. I prayed, "Just tell me what I need to do, and I'll do it." Have you ever heard the worldly phrase "Be careful what you ask for"? Well, I can tell you I got more than I bargained for when I was praying. As I was praying, all I could hear in my head was *sell, sell, sell!* As certain as I was the day I met my wife that God had sent her into my life, I was just as certain that I needed to sell my practice.

Thus, one week to the day after I had told my wife that I would never sell my practice and move . . . we left church, got into our car, and I looked at her and said, "How would you like to live closer to your family?" She replied, "You know that answer." I told her, "God has laid on my heart that I need to sell my office." I was so certain before we even left the church parking lot I called the young doctor and left this message, "Don't ask any questions because I surely don't have any answers; I know what I said three days ago, but if you want to buy a practice, I'm willing to look at that option." He called three minutes later, incredulous: "Are you kidding me? My wife and I just finished praying at church for God to open a door of opportunity if he wanted us to move to your town. I walked out and there was your message." How awesome is God? He orchestrated everything.

Going Nowhere according to God's Perfect Timing

Well to make a long story longer, he bought the practice, and we immediately put our house up for sale. I felt really good about it because I had peacefulness within me that I was following God's plan and not my own. I told my staff that I was selling the practice and that God had another plan for me; I did not know exactly what it was, but it was to be global. Many friends and patients thought I was crazy to sell my practice and home, especially since it was at the time of the real estate crash. Our house continued to sit on the market for about a year. I was beginning to think that God was testing me like Abraham, but I did not have another ram to sacrifice. At least the testimony about him in Hebrews 11:8 fit: "By faith Abraham, when called to go to a place he would later receive as his inheritance, obeyed and went, even though he did not know where he was going." As we continued to be patient, my wife and I were getting annoyed because we had already prepared ourselves mentally to leave and move to the town where we felt God had called us to live. This was all a matter of trusting Him and His timing in our lives.

My wife started praying to God to show us why we were still waiting to move. She informed me on a Sunday morning that she had had a dream the night before about someone wanting to buy our house at nine o'clock on Monday morning. Precisely at 8:45 a.m. on Monday, she walked into my office with the announcement, "Look at the clock. A realtor just called and wants to show the house today at one o'clock."

This showing happened to be to the person who was to buy our house. We needed to be out of the house within a month, prompting us to go to find a home in our new town. As we talked to the banks, we found that none of them was willing to use any of my available sources of income for us to purchase a home because they had not been established for more than two years. However, they said they could use the sale of my business. In order to use the sale of the business as income, I needed to have twelve months proof of payments. The day before we closed on our home I received my twelfth payment. We had no idea previously that this would be an issue, though in hindsight it was apparent that God certainly did.

God's timing is always perfect. God does not do things with mediocrity. He does things with excellence and perfection . . . in *His* eyes, not necessarily our own. Since we have moved to our new home, God has set our feet on paths that are putting us in directions we would not be headed had we not listened and continued to wait on Gods timing. In Psalm 27:14 (NKJV) we are encouraged to "wait on the LORD; be of good courage, and He shall strengthen your heart; wait, I say, on the LORD!" As you can see from the story above, God's fingerprint was everywhere in our story; He was paying attention to all the details and making sure everything was in its proper place. I just had to be obedient to *His* calling in my life.

It is important to move on God's Word and exercise the "muscle" of obedience because we are His vessels, here to thrive in life and spread His message of love to the ends of the earth (1 Cor. 4, esp. v. 7). The more we listen and take action, the more spiritually mature we become. I have noted previously that when one part of the body suffers all parts of the body suffer, and that when we do not move on the Lord's prompting we are not only delaying God's message but also are failing His people. This is a huge burden to bear, but with privilege comes responsibility. We must be careful how we live, not only because our lifestyle determines our righteousness— that it's to be judged—but also because it will impact our ability to hear from God, affecting those around us.

John wrote in Revelation 5:12, "In a loud voice they sang: 'Worthy is the Lamb, who was slain, to receive power and wealth and wisdom and strength and honor and glory and praise!'" Let's be sure in all our actions that we are giving reverence to the Lord and obeying His commands, according His written Word, as we give Him the praise, glory, and honor. Let's be fully submitted to His power, wealth, wisdom, and strength as we humbly depend upon the Holy Spirit for our guidance. Let's move for Him!

Physical Movement

Our bodies were designed to move. God gave us our own systems of built-in intelligence that prompt us to move and keep us active. However, in general we consciously suppress that intelligence. The Industrial Revolution brought sweeping changes in many areas of life, including the family, work, and society. Perhaps no other factor has contributed more to establishing the sedentary nature of people's lifestyles and work ever since, explaining in large part why we are less active today. Today, life is easier and more convenient than ever before. We have computers, cell phones, cars, remote controls, home delivery services, and new technologies emerging all the time. These modern conveniences of today have become our postmodern inconveniences of tomorrow with regard at least to our physical health.

Oftentimes when people are looking for an exception in the Bible with regard to their poor lifestyle choices, they will say, "Well, the Bible is not very clear on such and such, since it does not talk much about that subject." The Bible has guidance for every area of our lives. It may not talk at length on some topics, but with the Holy Spirit and often the input of godly mentors, we are usually able to discern what is best for us. One of the most common subjects on which people believe the Bible is unclear is physical exercise.

Here's where the key verse I mentioned earlier comes into play: "For physical training is of some value, but godliness has value for all things, holding promise for both the present life and the life to come" (1 Tim. 4:8). Notice that Paul does not deny the need for exercise. Rather, he says that exercise is valuable. However, the Bible prioritizes exercise correctly by saying that godliness is of greater value. This Scripture points out that "Godliness has value for all things," and this includes our health. As pointed out in chapter 6, the mind controls the body, and our mind is either controlled by our will or by God's will. If we let God's good, pleasing, and perfect will reign in our lives (Rom. 12:2), we will create the best conditions to promote health and healing in our whole body.

We have learned that our bodies consist of both physical and spiritual components that exist as a unified entity in the being of a human person—and that we are not to neglect either one. Throughout his epistles the apostle Paul uses athletic terminology to teach us spiritual truths. From my perspective this indicates that Paul viewed physical exercise, and even competition, in a positive light. Paul says,

> Do you not know that in a race all the runners run, but only one gets the prize? Run in such a way as to get the prize. Everyone who competes in the games goes into strict training. They do it to get a crown that will not last, but we do it to get a crown that will last forever. Therefore I do not run like someone running aimlessly; I do not fight like a boxer beating the air. No, I strike a blow to my body and make it my slave so that after I have preached to others, I myself will not be disqualified for the prize. (1 Cor. 9:24–27)

Paul equates the Christian life to a race we run to "get the prize." The prize we seek is not gold or silver or bronze but an eternal crown that will not tarnish nor fade. Are you in strict training to achieve this prize?

Staying Inspired

Why should we use physical exercise as a way to care for ourselves? We *shouldn't*. I believe we should partake in physical exercise to be an optimal, holy dwelling for the Lord and to be better able to love our neighbor as we share God's love. The parable of the Good Samaritan in Luke 10:25–37 can provide us with further insight. An expert of the law asked Jesus, "What must I do to inherit eternal life?" Jesus responded to him with the question, "What is written in the Law? How do you read it?" The legal expert responded, "Love the Lord your God with all your heart and with all your soul and with all your strength and with all your mind; and love your neighbor as yourself." Jesus said to the man that he was correct, but the man was confused as to who was considered his neighbor.

This is where Jesus gave the parable. In the parable there were two men who walked by on the other side of the road past the man who had been robbed and nearly beaten to death. It is clear that these two men, despite their impeccable religious credentials, were not right *spiritually*. On the other hand, the third man walked up to the beaten man, inconvenienced himself by stopping, and cared for him and his wounds. Then he took him to an inn and paid for the expenses the innkeeper would incur during the victim's convalescence. It is obvious the third man was not only right spiritually but was also properly equipped to take action and help the man.

If we do not have a reserve of energy we will not be able to help those in need. If we don't have a reserve of endurance at the end of a stressful day, we will find ourselves drained and are likely to plop on the couch and do nothing to help a neighbor. If we are depressed, thinking only of ourselves, we are not going to think to help our neighbor. If we fill our schedule with too many activities, we will be too busy to notice or acknowledge the needs of our neighbors, and we will not help them. If we become slothful and lazy we will miss opportunities to share the love of God. Now you might be asking, "How do I get this surplus of energy?"

Physical Exercise and Its Mental Health Benefits

We have talked about the benefits of being right with God's will at the core of our heart, as this provides us with the inspiration to go into training in all aspects of our life. This will lead to eating the proper foods and so ingesting the nutrients that our body was designed to have for functionality. Equipped with these two components in place, we are left with integrating movement into our lives to take proper care and optimize the use of the Lord's vessel, our body.

Exercise can increase by 300 percent the enzymes inside the energy producing organelles in our bodies called mitochondria. Additionally, simple exercises can double the number of mitochondria (energy producers) per cell.[99] If you were to do the math, you'd find that the sum equals a 600 percent increase in energy production, just from simple exercise. So there you have it. How do we get an overabundance of energy to be better equipped to help and love your neighbor? Through exercise. No wonder the mitochondria are called the powerhouse of the cell! How awesome is God's design? The more energy we expend, the more energy we make.

Exercise has even been shown to have a positive influence on mental health. Dr. Daniel M. Landers stated, "We now have evidence to support the claim that exercise is related to positive mental health as indicated by relief in symptoms of depression and anxiety."[100] The trend in Western medicine is to put people on drugs, such as antidepressants, when they suffer from depressive illnesses. Some say that there are enough antidepressants prescribed every day in America for every man, woman, and child to have one pill a day. That's a lot of antidepressants! Do you think God created our body to need all those antidepressants? No, not at all. I do believe they can be beneficial in an emergency situation, as long as the person is making efforts to make their situation better as they become more focused on God, so His healing power can take precedence and remove the need for the prescription medication.

Research shows that exercise is just as effective as antidepressants. If doctors are going to recommend putting something into the body that will inhibit a function of the body for symptomatic relief, shouldn't the drug—which has potential side effects—be *more effective* if we're going to prescribe it to anyone? Study after study has shown that exercise promotes mental health and reduces symptoms of depression. The antidepressant effect of regular physical exercise is comparable to that of the potent antidepressants. It may take at least thirty minutes of exercise a day for at least three to five days a week to significantly improve symptoms of depression.[101]

What is more interesting is that the more we exercise, the better effect it has on depression and anxiety.[102] This means that we need to increase our dose of exercise, not our dose of medication, to assist us in our times of depression and anxiety. Some of you may be saying, *When I'm depressed I don't feeling like exercising.* This is precisely the time when we need to depend upon the Holy Spirit living in us to give us the power to move. I believe this can effectively be done if we switch our focus from ourselves and appropriately direct it onto our Lord and Savior.

The *Journal of Applied Physiology* says, "Clearly, there is a solution to this epidemic of metabolic diseases that is inundating today's societies worldwide: exercise and diet."[103] A new dietary approach, along with moderate exercise, would have a major impact in controlling and actually lowering the costs of medical care.[104] Exercise has many benefits; it has even been shown to help reduce one's appetite. Imagine this: with simple exercise you can remove the effects of depression, thereby removing the tendency to turn to comfort food, thus giving you clarity of mind so you can better focus and listen for God's will for your life.

We Were Made to Move

As I have said, we are made to move. Research from Clinical Biomechanics in 1987 states, "Evidence shows beyond reasonable doubt that immobilization (lack of movement) is not only a cause of osteoarthritis but that it delays healing." Let's rephrase that statement: lack of movement causes us to break down and hinders our ability to heal. Exercise can help us fight infections by stimulating our immune system.[105] It can help us avoid blood sugar issues such as Type II Diabetes.[106] Additionally, exercise can enhance the strength of our bones, which will help us to avoid osteoporosis.[107] The benefits of exercise are endless, and so is the research to back those benefits. The main point is for us to recognize that when our life if fully aligned with the Word of God we will have health in our whole body.

We don't have to work out for an hour every day. If we simply put in thirty to forty-five minutes most days of the week, we will make progressive gains in our health. It has been scientifically proven that small daily workouts will improve our health more effectively than a long workout a few days a week.[108] If you cannot currently exercise every day, some exercise is better than no exercise to counteract a sedentary lifestyle. If you are unable to move physically, perhaps due to an injury, you can still move spiritually on God's Word.

The dosage of exercise is important. If we are simply jogging or walking briskly to regain our health, this is not enough if our wish to accelerate the healing process. Paul said, "Everyone who competes in the games goes into strict training." (1 Cor. 9:25). It is all about *frequency*, *duration*, and *intensity*. The more frequently we do something, and the longer and more intensely we do it, the bigger and better the changes in our life. This applies not only to our physical health but also to our spiritual health.

We must remember that if we allow ourselves to be spiritual weaklings, it will be hard for us to discern God's voice calling in our lives, especially if we haven't learned to recognize what it sounds like. Nor can we move correctly on the promptings or "feelings" in our lives if we cannot check them against the Bible to see if the prompting is from the Lord, Satan, or just ourselves. Finally, we cannot fight the enemy with the utterance of the Word of God if we do not know the Word of God.

This is where spiritual fitness comes in. In order to achieve victory over the enemy and be thriving vessels, ready to do the good works he has prepared in advance for us to do (Eph. 2:10), we must study God's Word with focus and repetition throughout all our days. This can include reading through the Bible, memorizing and meditating on Scripture, learning to pray the Scriptures back to God, and other ways of engrafting Scripture into our lives. The more frequently we do it, and the longer and more intensely we do it, the more solidly His purpose, grace, and power will reign in our lives. Jesus' prayer to His Father in heaven expresses what our hearts' attitude needs to be every day: "Not my will, but yours be done" (Luke 22:42; cf. Matt. 6:10).

Enough But Not Too Much

As with many things in life, there are extremes in all areas, to the point of gluttony, and exercise is not exempt. Some people exercise too much and eat too little for reasons of vanity—what is beautiful and good-looking, as our culture defines beauty, is too often empty and devoid of what really matters. You know "the look"—we're bombarded with these images every day. We do judge, not only the book by its cover, but also people by how they look rather than by the content of their character and the moral worth of their deeds. Others eat properly but focus too much on the shape of their physical bodies, and they neglect their spiritual growth, thus becoming spiritual weaklings. Our culture worships youth and undervalues the wisdom of the aged, and we get caught up with pursuing what glitters but does not last.

The wisdom of God offers a healthy corrective, along with a little dose of reality therapy: "Charm is deceptive, and beauty is fleeting; but a woman who fears the LORD is to be praised" (Prov. 31:30) Likewise, "the glory of young men is their strength, gray hair the splendor of the old" (Prov. 20:29). Youth is a gift quickly spent and thus not to be wasted: "Remember your Creator in the days of your youth, before the days of trouble come and the years approach when you will say, 'I find no pleasure in them'" (Eccles. 12:1). However, on the flip side, some people focus only on spiritual fitness as they neglect their physical bodies. None of these scenarios resembles a fully aligned, balanced life, according to God's Word.

Remember in chapter 3 where I said that we shouldn't abstain from eating to be thin or exercise to look fit; that our thoughts shouldn't be of personal gain? This is true, and God warns against vanity a number of times in the Bible. In 1 Samuel 16:7 we read God's instructions to Samuel regarding His choice of Israel's first king: "Do not consider his appearance or his height, for I have rejected him. The LORD does not look at the things man looks at. Man looks at the outward appearance, but the LORD looks at the heart." Proverbs 31:30 states, "Charm is deceptive, and beauty is fleeting; but a woman who fears the LORD is to be praised." And 1 Peter 3:3–4 declares, "Your beauty should not come from outward adornment, such as elaborate hairstyles and the wearing of gold jewelry or fine clothes. Rather, it should be that of your inner self, the unfading beauty of a gentle and quiet spirit, which is of great worth in God's sight." The goal of exercising should be to improve our physical and mental health so we will possess more physical energy when we get the prompt from God to act in faith on His behalf.

Embodied Now and Forever to Glorify and Enjoy God

We are never going to be one hundred percent perfect in our physical makeup, according to what we may desire. So if we are focusing on some unrealistic ideal, we are caught up in on our own selfish desires rather than in Christ. In the previous chapter I said that our memory has no ability to relive satisfaction in a way that prevents us from needing repeated doses of whatever it is that has provided us comfort. We need to focus on God and resist vanity because we may never be satisfied with our bodies; it is the Living Water (Jesus) that alone satisfies our true thirst (John 4:10, 13–14).

Few statements summarize the proper focus for life better than the first question and answer of the Westminster Shorter Catechism: "What is the chief end of man? Man's chief end is to glorify God, and to enjoy Him forever." Paul says in Philippians 3:21, "He will take our weak mortal bodies and change them into glorious bodies like his own, using the same power with which he will bring everything under his control." The effects of sin are hard on the body, causing it to break down and eventually die. Because the first man sinned and brought death into the world, what is written about Adam is what every one of us someday must face (give or take a few centuries!): "Altogether, Adam lived 930 years, and then he died" (Gen. 5:5).

Yet God intended not death but life—life that is full and free, without sin, disease, and death to drag us down (John 10:10; Rev. 7:17; 21:4; 22:1–5). Embodied existence in the world to come, after God makes all things new, without the effects and limitations of sin, is something every Christian should anticipate. We will have perfection when we receive our heavenly reward. In order for us to have that, He instructs us to be strong spiritually and physically to serve His purpose by sharing His love. Christian theology professor and author Gregg Allison (the professor mentioned in the introduction) reconciles nicely the physical and spiritual aspects of what it means to be human, to be embodied, and to live in God's world as His people:

> As divine image bearers created for embodied existence both now and in eternity, we do well to live our human embodiment cognizant of the rich instruction given in Scripture. . . . Whether we are confronting questions from people experiencing physical problems, addressing the uniqueness of human genderedness and sexuality, struggling personally with gluttony or sloth, selecting clothes to wear, expressing our worship through physical acts, praying for the sick, or pondering the mystery of the life to come, Scripture provides abundant teaching that corrects wrongful attitudes toward the body and underscores the wonderful reality of human embodiment.[109]

This gives all of us plenty to think about. We've lived far too long with that familiar but false Gnostic dualism from Greek philosophy called Platonism, which says that the spirit is good but matter is evil. Too many of my patients are practical Platonists who trash their bodies and pop pills to suppress their symptoms. They are like the patient I mentioned in the introduction whose words I can't forget: "I guess I'm not sick enough yet to make the lifestyle changes you ask of me, but I'll be back when I am."

Plato was wrong about this.[18] The body and the spirit were not created evil but were created by God to be united in a being who, though a creature, yet mirrors in many ways the Creator's own image and likeness—a situation or state God said was "very good" (Gen. 1:26–27, 31; 2:7). Could there be any greater affirmation of the human body than what God did through the incarnation of His Son: "And the Word became flesh and made his dwelling [tabernacled] among us"? (John 1:14). Since then, Jesus has been disembodied only once (Luke 23:46), but never again will His spirit be separated from His body (Acts 2:24; Heb. 7:16). Unfortunately, the church has long perpetuated Plato's teaching in many ways. It's time to slough off not the human body but our wrong views of the body and instead take care of our bodies, optimizing our physical potential for health and healing so we can serve God well in body and soul, full of faith and of His Spirit, ready to do His will in the world.[110]

Being Sick Well

This is all fine and good if you're basically healthy and just need to improve on your eating and exercising habits. But what about those who suffer from various diseases or chronic illnesses, since the number of people facing such problems is growing? One thing that can encourage us is knowing that God designed life, including our body and its ability to heal itself, to work well. Although it is true, as we said earlier, that sins such as bitterness and lack of forgiveness can cause illness, as evidently was the case in the early church regarding the Lord's Supper (1 Cor. 11:27–30). But when personal sin is not at issue, we have to understand human disease and sickness as part of the broader human condition that includes the consequences of living in a world fallen due to humanity's long-ago moral rebellion against God (Gen. 3).

Thus it is no exaggeration to suggest that all physical evil, including all types of disease, communicable or noncommunicable, is a consequence of moral evil.[111] For example, God did not genetically program us to become sick. However, there are children born with genetic disorders that yield disease. *Why would God do that?* we're prone to ask. But who are we, I counter, to say that these illnesses are caused by God, that they aren't, for example, side effects from toxic chemicals being leaked into the ground water by a greedy company trying to save a few dollars? An unsuspecting mother drinks the poisoned water and unwittingly passes along genetic abnormalities to the developing child within her womb.

I believe the movie *Erin Brockovich* does a nice job of displaying the physical consequences of moral evil. Obviously, illegal dumping practices are only one of many environmental factors negatively affecting people's health today. But many other factors are part of the very structure and pattern of life in America: how food is grown, what foods we choose to eat, the prescriptions we take, and many other lifestyle behaviors that, if altered, could improve, if not eliminate, many of our health problems.

In any case, there is hope for those who choose to change their lifestyle. Likewise, because of God's grace, chronic illness doesn't have to rule people's lives or the lives of those who care for them.[112] This is another example of keeping in step with the movement of Scripture, in terms of how we respond to the unevenness of life in our attitudes, values, and faith in God, whatever providence he brings.

In the book of Daniel, it was not the fact that Daniel and his three friends looked healthier and better nourished that was pleasing to God. It was the fact that their hearts were focused on His will, a centering that brought peace and health to their bodies (Prov. 14:30). Aware of the meaning of his name ("God is my judge"), Daniel knew that God wanted his heart and that he would be judged accordingly. Daniel's heart-focus on God is what gave him that bone-deep resolve to consistently live with integrity, and he did not fall prey to the daily temptations to become a Babylonian. A heart that is submitted to God, knowing Him to be in control, and obeys the Lord has no difficulty making the right decisions. Daniel is a perfect example of how God's blessings are bestowed upon us as we resist being conformed to the ways of this world. When he had to choose between the Babylonian culture and God's Word, this young man chose God's Word. Daniel was indeed a transformer, and we should be too; if not, we risk perishing at the hands of our fast-paced, stressed-out modern society.

If we lose the momentum to go to work for Him every day because we're too fatigued to get out of bed, how are we going to serve our purpose? Sometimes our life gets so busy that we forget to "be still" and listen to God's prompting. When this occurs, we slowly start to edge God out of the core of our hearts, only to later find ourselves sitting there aimlessly again. Many times we may have direction from God, but many of us don't act upon it because we are busy, tired, or timid.

However, we are called to do better than that. In 2 Timothy 1:7 Paul says, "For God did not give us a spirit of timidity, but a spirit of power, of love and of self-discipline." We are running the race to share God's love with the world through the gifts He has blessed each of us with. Without a purpose for our lives, what would be the point of caring for ourselves? We've got to have something bigger than ourselves on which to focus. However, we are not going to know our purpose unless we know Him through His Word, listen for Him, and move according to His promptings. When we do that, health will be restored to His temple. "Therefore, since we are surrounded by such a great cloud of witnesses, let us throw off everything that hinders and the sin that so easily entangles. And let us run with perseverance the race marked out for us" (Heb. 12:1).

CHAPTER 9

The Bottom Line

"Do not be deceived: God cannot be mocked. A man reaps what he sows. The one who sows to please his flesh, from the flesh will reap destruction; the one who sows to please the Spirit, from the Spirit will reap eternal life."

Galatians 6:7–8

"There can be no true response without responsibility; there can be no responsibility without response."

Arthur Vogel

Here is the bottom line: *is an honor and privilege to house the Holy Spirit of God within us.* We may not think about this very much, but the Creator and Lord of the universe has chosen to dwell in jars of clay, mere earthen vessels, human forms shaped from dust and animated by the breath of life from God, earthly tent to dwell in during the limited days of our lives. British Christian singer-songwriter and worship leader Graham Kendrick expressed beautifully in song this wonderful paradox:

Lord of eternity dwells in humanity . . .

Lifts our humanity to the heights of His throne.
O what a mystery, meekness and majesty,
Bow down and worship for this is your God.[113]

In response we ask with the psalmist, "What is man that you are mindful of him, the son of man that you care for him?" (Ps. 8:4; cf. Heb. 2:6).

Freedom in Christ and Gospel-Shaped, Healthy Living

Ultimately, we who believe in Jesus are responsible to fulfill God's good purpose in our generation. The gospel of Jesus Christ sets the agenda for the church. As we worship God we work for the growth of His kingdom, which is extended throughout the world and advances through the proclamation of the good news about Jesus Christ, coupled with the sharing of Christ's love to all people in every generation. The visible demonstration of God's love in and through His people is what will separate the truth from the lies of our culture. I've busted a lot of healthcare myths over the years, and there is no shortage of false and misleading information still out there. The gospel applies to all areas of life and truth. Therefore we cannot forget that underlying all else we can offer to others (including all the various goals and plans we may have for ourselves), our existence on earth is about bringing people *life* through Christ—the Truth.

In order for this to occur optimally, we must first have freedom . . . freedom of thought; freedom of emotion; freedom of movement; and, as much as possible, freedom from ailment—

whether spiritual, mental, emotional, chemical, or physical. What is freedom? Freedom is not the ability to do whatever we want but the right or the power to do what we ought to do. In Galatians 5:1 Paul says, "It is for freedom that Christ has set us free." Likewise, in 2 Corinthians 3:17 the apostle emphasizes God's part: "Now the Lord is the Spirit, and where the Spirit of the Lord is, there is freedom." Through this freedom come the peace and joy promised to us from God when we let His will reign in our lives (Rom. 14:17; 15:13; Phil. 4:4–9).

As this gift of freedom is received and growth in God's grace occurs within us, we will increasingly be empowered to share God's love beyond what we ever thought possible, as the love poured into our hearts by the Holy Spirit overflows for God and people. All of this is made possible by the freedom God gives us in Christ Jesus from the penalty and power of sin through Jesus' suffering and death on the cross, His resurrection from the dead, and His ascension as exalted King into heaven (Acts 1:9–11; Rom. 8:1–4; 1 Cor. 15:3–4). This is the freedom that the gospel of Jesus Christ brings to those who were enslaved in sin. In connection with His Father's mission, Jesus Himself proclaimed liberty for the captives (Luke 4:18; cf. Isa. 61:1). If we obey Jesus, we have this promise from Him: "If the Son sets you free, you will be free indeed" (John 8:36). Only Jesus can set us free in all the ways we need it.

By His Resurrection We Are Healed

The gospel tells us that Jesus died for our sins, was buried, and was raised on the third day, all according to the Scriptures (1 Cor. 15:3). The resurrection of Jesus from the dead has had a ripple effect throughout all creation and is the death blow to death itself, including all human disorders and diseases. The resurrection of Jesus Christ from the dead is clearly first of all about God's redemption of all things, including His offer to every human being to receive eternal life through His only Son by the Holy Spirit (Col. 1:19–22); but Jesus' resurrection is also our ultimate hope for being healed of all our sicknesses and diseases, even as physicians and patients together do what they can to pursue health, healing, and faith. It is one thing to believe in the eventual resurrection of the dead, sometime in the future, at the last day; it is quite another to believe that Jesus is the Christ, the Son of God, who came into the world and who said, "I am the resurrection and the life. He who believes in me will live, even though he dies, and whoever lives and believes in me will never die. Do you believe this?" (John 11:24–27). It was very soon afterward that Jesus raised his friend Lazarus from the grave! (vv. 43–44).

In an article sketching out a theology of wellness, James Morgante, a chaplain working in the healthcare sector, emphasized the significance of the resurrection of Christ with regard to the healings Jesus performed, as recorded in the Gospels:

Jesus' healing ministry signified the overcoming of disease, sin, and the evil that stood behind them. And yet the final resolution of the problem they pose is not the healings themselves but the Resurrection, which signifies victory over death—death being the most serious manifestation of disease, sin, and evil. Healing disease and restoring health in the Gospel narratives are transitional steps to the ultimate goal of a complete and permanent cure through the Resurrection.[114]

Someday when God makes all things new, we'll also be free from the presence of sin, never again to feel its pull, which for now Christians do experience as the remaining corruption of sinful habits from the old life before coming to faith in Jesus Christ, who gives life to our mortal bodies (Rom. 8:11; Rev. 21:1–5).

Receiving freedom and healing from God can sometimes come in the form of what we call a "miracle" or a "spontaneous healing." Make no mistake: God has the ability to perform such works—after all, He is God. Divine healing is one of those areas that requires faith to receive—or faith to endure if in God's providence healing is not granted in this way, despite our desires and prayers. Oftentimes God asks us to be an active participant in achieving our liberation from disease and destructive lifestyle habits as we build our relationship with Him. These journeys to achieve freedom can take time, sometimes a long time, and we must persevere. With slavery comes a certain mentality, which I described in chapter 5 of the book. Old habits die hard, but we must keep trying to unlearn the old ways of doing things and learn the new habits of health, healing (physical, mental, emotional, and spiritual), and faith.

Do We Value Our Life?

Our ability to persevere will depend in part on the value we put on our life. Life is God's gift, along with the space and time to live it. We will never be different from the rest of the world around us if we do not value our life. From this point forward we need to define *value* in terms of seeing ourselves through God's eyes. Human beings are His creation; we are here for His purpose, . . . and, stunningly, we are His most precious possession. A biblical Christian view of life in our current world requires that we put value on our health and not on a lifestyle that tends toward sickness.

There's another way of seeing all of this—in terms of an age-old battle. Satan, God's enemy and the enemy of every son and daughter of Adam and Eve, is against our surviving, let alone thriving. The last thing he wants is for people to live fully and freely as image-bearing human beings, renewed in knowledge in the image of our Creator (Col. 3:10; 2 Cor. 4:16). He hates God and thus hates us. So realizing that health has a spiritual dimension helps us to look with compassion on the people of the world in all their distress and disease, to see them as the Savior did, in need of God's healing touch and saving grace. Our actions display our values.

This may mean intentionally choosing to pay close attention to the rebuke and correction of God's Word and to counter the deceptive, negative, and unhealthy thoughts that can creep into our minds but are not of the Lord. It may mean choosing to stand alone, like Daniel and his three friends, at church potlucks and picnics and making healthful choices whenever we eat. It may also mean choosing to schedule physical activity, especially if we live a mostly sedentary lifestyle. Finally, it may mean getting out of our comfort zone and moving upon God's promptings. Certainly the principle of moderation comes into play in our world of extreme excesses; there's a difference between indulging in a piece of cake at a wedding and having one daily for dessert. The point is that we need to be intentional about what we think; what we eat; how we move; and why, as well as how, all of this affects our bodies.

What it comes down to is that if we value God's vision of who we are and what we are to do, then we must be proactive in the care of His creation, His temples, His dwellings, His vessels. This is a holistic calling. In terms of Christian ministry, as someone has put it, this is the whole gospel for the whole person for the whole world. God wants to minister to both our soul/spirit and our body. Putting this in terms of our broken healthcare system, one way forward is to affirm an approach that focuses on health and acknowledges the whole human being, as well as following Jesus' example, as Morgante suggests:

> [In] the debate between holistic medicine (with its emphasis on prevention) versus physical medicine (with an emphasis on intervention), . . . the Judeo-Christian tradition resolves the question of intervention or prevention by supporting *both* at the same time. The laws governing health illustrate the prevention-oriented side. Yet Jesus, who discourages sin and encourages faith, is also the archetype of the intervening physician who heals in order "to manifest God's works"—God's will to heal—while also raising the question of whether any cure can last without the living faith in God that serves to protect health.[115]

This message of health, healing, and faith is for everyone, but especially for God's people in the church today. Our calling is to set an example for the world in all areas of life, demonstrating just how completely Jesus Christ can transform people's lives spiritually, chemically, mentally, emotionally, and physically. But this requires our cooperation, also known as patient compliance. We are called to "walk by faith" and this implies that we are to have movement, to take action and be compliant to our Lord's commands. Dr. Tony Evans, in his sermon "Discovering the Strength of Faith," said it well: "If you have faith but you have no movement, faith is not what you have. You may have a bunch of things, but if your feet are still, you don't have faith, you have feelings and emotions."[116] We need to move beyond feelings and emotions, to truly *live* by faith so healing can occur, so we can be made whole through the Lord who heals and enables us to live life to the full.

Taking Responsibility for Our Lifestyle and Health

We must hold each other accountable, as brothers and sisters in Christ, to care for God's vessel, our body, so we can optimally serve His purpose. The word *accountability* can be defined as "an obligation or willingness to accept responsibility or to account for one's actions."[117] It is not only a privilege to be a vessel in which the Spirit of Christ dwells; it was also an incredible privilege to have Jesus die on the cross for our sins. However, with this privilege comes responsibility. In Luke 12:48 Jesus is recorded as saying, "From everyone who has been given much, much will be demanded; and from the one who has been entrusted with much, much more will be asked." And in 2 Timothy 1:14 we read, "Guard the good deposit that was entrusted to you—guard it with the help of the Holy Spirit who lives in us." Caring for the Lord's "sanctuary" is to be a team effort. We cannot separate our responsibilities to God and the church, the body of Christ, from our actions because the two go hand in hand. Remember, when one person suffers, everyone suffers; when one rejoices, everyone rejoices (1 Cor. 12:26).

It is true that we are all human, but once any of us accepts Christ into our lives we are able to live for God by the power of the Holy Spirit within us. However, we have to choose if we are going to live by His power dwelling within us or by our own willpower. Utilizing the power of the Holy Spirit, who lives in us, is a constant choice. Let us give it all to God, live by faith, and truly submit ourselves to the leading of the Holy Spirit, because walking by our own wisdom and power is scary and sure to fail. As we rely upon the Holy Spirit to drown out the many voices calling us to conform to the patterns of this world, health and peace will be brought to the whole body.

Each of us is at a different level of health and blessed with different abilities, but no matter where we are on these continuums we can dedicate ourselves to contribute to God's kingdom by working at our full potential. "Each one should use whatever gift he has received to serve others, faithfully administering God's grace in its various forms" (1 Peter 4:10). We need to optimally develop and use the gifts we have been blessed with by God. Let us live in the fullness of the life we were created for!

Believe in and value who God created you to be because you are God's vessel. Live in such a way that others can't miss the vibrancy, peace, and joy in your life as you actively pursue ways to honor and live in the truth, empowered by the Holy Spirit. Let Him completely transform you in every area of your life. "For the kingdom of God is not a matter of eating and drinking, but of righteousness, peace and joy in the Holy Spirit" (Rom. 14:17).

At one time or another the Holy Spirit has convicted each of us about the wrongs in our lives, whether or not we are yet believers in Christ. Jesus said, "When [the Holy Spirit] comes, he will convict the world of guilt in regard to sin and righteousness and judgment: in regard to sin, because men do not believe in me; in regard to righteousness, because I am going to the Father, where you can see me no longer; and in regard to judgment, because the prince of this world now stands condemned" (John 16:8–11). From the thoughts we think to the food choices we make to our levels of physical activity to our lack of movement upon the Word to obey Christ by the Spirit's promptings—we have all been pricked in our conscience about our errors and sinful habits.

It is important to note that the Scripture teaches us to know the good we are supposed to do; if we don't then do it, we sin (James 4:17). Thus, when we stock up on the knowledge of truth without applying it, we are in fact sinning. Likewise, the apostle Paul said, "Everything that does not come from faith is sin" (Rom. 14:23). This may seem pretty obvious when it comes to believing a doctrine (e.g., that Jesus was both fully divine and fully human). But how does putting God's truth into practice work out in terms of making healthy choices about the thoughts we think, the foods we eat today, or the decisions to be physically active and move upon God's Word?

Is there such a thing as thinking and eating ethically or Christianly? How about regular exercise as stewardship of one's body?[118] Formulating a Christian ethic to guide our choice of foods to eat certainly depends on a number of factors, such as our budget, the availability of and our access to nourishing foods, food sensitivities or allergies, personal nutritional needs, and so on. I pray that we not only accept the knowledge of God's truth but that we also apply it to our lives. Empowered by the Holy Spirit, let us confess, grow, and change into the people God created us to be.

My dear brothers and sisters, we are called to do work for the Lord, and there is much work for us to do as God works in us and through us. Let us become His willing vessels, and let us live by the power of the Holy Spirit to become an unstoppable force for spreading God's love to the ends of the earth and through the end of time. Let us not waste time. Let the transformation begin now because the world needs us and God wants us. The world does not need you or me as half a person, living well below our potential; our world and the church need us whole, completely equipped with the Holy Spirit, ready, willing, and able to do the will of God.

Acknowledgments

I n my first book, *Sex, Lies, and Cholesterol*, I did not write an acknowledgments section because it seemed daunting to recognize all the people who have helped shape me throughout my life, and I did not want to leave anyone out. However, this book has been a long project (over five years), and many people have directly and indirectly influenced its content and deserve recognition. So here goes.

I am deeply grateful for the life that God has given me. From the trials and tribulations in my life to the successes and achievements, I am grateful for them all. I am most thankful for God's guidance and never-ending love and for using me to help His vessels thrive by publishing the important message of this book for everyone, but especially for His people, the church.

Without the support, encouragement, tireless hours, and honesty of my wife, Terra, this book would have never seen the light of day. Your discernment, honesty, and positive influence have helped shape this book to send the right practical message. I am so blessed to have you in my life, and I love chasing our dreams and God's will for our lives together. This book has been a great achievement in my life, but my greatest will always be living my life with you as one. I love you.

To my children, Reese, Ella, and Haden, thank you for all your patience as I have worked so long on this book, thank you for all the meals Mom prepared for you to bring into my office, and thank you for following Mom and Dad's prompting from the Lord to pick up and move to a different state. Thank you for teaching me so much about life. I love being your daddy, and I couldn't possibly love you "too much."

There are some people other than my wife to whom I owe special thanks for the early developmental edits of content and proofing of this book. My family's dear friend Jennifer Roudebush for her efforts in proofing; my sister Barbra Bentley for her editing, ideas, and honest opinions about the content and how it inspired her; my longtime friend Chris Knott for his theological insights and additions to the content; David Weil for his thoughts regarding content and his earnest prayers for my life; Bryndon Preston for his unbounded encouragement and prayer; Marcie Shrom for her input on honing in on my message in the introduction; Gayle Duer for helping me organize a class at our church that led to the creation and content of this book; and, finally, Alan Seaborn for all the hours you have listened to me read my content after our morning workouts and for your theological and practical insights. I am very thankful to you all.

To my new team and friends at Credo Communications, you are all unbelievable. Tim Beals, thank you for seeing the need of this message and helping to bring it to the world. Paul Brinkerhoff, you have truly "put the icing on the cake" with the skill set you have been blessed with (sorry for using such a sugarcoated saying in a health book)—thank you for all your effort, time, and research to make this book complete. I have deep respect for my team at Credo—thank you all.

To my business partners, friends, and brothers in Christ, I am forever blessed to have you in my life. Thank you for all your encouraging words and for seeing my many business visions—I love you all: Aaron Oxenrider, Andy Robbins, Bryndon Preston, and Shawn Benzinger.

I would like to thank the pastors who have had direct and great influence in my theological understanding of God's Word: Dan Seaborn, David Wigington, Paul Hontz, Tom Elsworth, and Steve Wesner. I would also like to thank all those with whom I have spent time studying and discussing God's Word in small groups.

This section is to those who have had great influence in my life and have helped shape who I have become as a person, thus indirectly contributing to this book. First to my parents, Martha Bentley and Roderick Bentley and to his wife Mary Bentley, thank you and I love you for all your love and support throughout the years as I continue to develop as a son, brother, friend, and father. I am grateful for my life and the pivotal roles you play in its development.

To my siblings, Deborah Dean, Roderick Bentley, Barbra Bentley, and Kristin Rushenberg, thank you for all your love, support, and for helping me to know, ever since I was a little boy, that I can do anything I put my mind to. I love you all.

To my in-laws, Sheryl and Chuck Wortinger, Dawn and Rob Fisher, and Troy and Kathy Carson: your incredible influence in my life has been unparalleled, as you've displayed how family love is unconditional and to be demonstrated no matter what the circumstances—thank you so much for allowing me to be part of your family.

To all my nieces and nephews (too many to name), thank you for letting me be "Uncle Ryan." I love you all deeply and cherish every moment with you.

I would like to say thank you and I love you to the entire Martin family, including the Kenkellen, Wirgua, and Nichols families. Thank you for your influence of faith and love that you have extended to my family. We love you.

To my closest friends I haven't already mentioned, with whom I have shared many life adventures and who have impacted my life significantly, I love you for your lifelong friendship and ability to pick up wherever we left off, no matter the length of time since our last communication: Craig Bowden and Rich and Myra Raake and family.

To my friends who are like family, whom I've been blessed to have as employees in my practice: Ashley Francke and Shelly Nelson. Thank you for all your love, support, and understanding as I transitioned in life and sold my practice to Dr. Hulbert to carry out God's will for my life. I appreciate and love both of you. Dr. Travis Hulbert and family, thank you for following God's will and listening to his calling. I am grateful for our friendship.

I would like to say thank you to some of my coaches who were especially influential men in my life as a teenager. It is because of these men that I learned to work hard for what I want to achieve, to never give up even when all seems hopeless, to give my best effort all the time, and to live by the quote attributed to Ralph Waldo Emerson: "Do not go where the path may lead; go instead where there is no path and leave a trail!" Thank you, Bill Roggeman, Matt Furfaro, and Tim Dawson.

I also want to offer a special note to thank those who were not specifically mentioned by name. To all my friends, family members, teachers, coaches, and patients, you have all helped influence my life story.

Notes

Introduction

1   Gregg R. Allison, "Toward a Theology of Human Embodiment," *Southern Baptist Journal of Theology* 13, no. 2 (Summer 2009): 1, http://www.sbts.edu/resources/files/2009/10/sbjt-2009summer-allison.pdf.

2   Kenneth D. Kochanek, Jiaquan Xu; Sherry L. Murphy, Arialdi M. Miniño, and Hsiang-Ching Kung, "Deaths: Final Data for 2009" *National Vital Statistics Reports* 60, no. 3 (December 29, 2011), 13, http://www.cdc.gov/nchs/data/nvsr/nvsr60/nvsr60_03.pdf.

3   Meridith Minkler, "Health Promotion at the Dawn of the 21st Century: Challenges and Dilemmas," *Promoting Human Wellness: New Frontiers for Research, Practice, and Policy*, ed. Margaret Schneider Jamner and Daniel Stokols (Berkeley: University of California Press, 2000), 350. Certainly the vision of health promotion today includes environmental and other factors known to contribute to toxicity levels related to, for example, food production, ground water, and the air we breathe, especially in the cities. Some people exhibit high degrees of sensitivity to such factors.

4   J. K. Iglehart, "From the Editor: Special Issue on Promoting Health," *Health Affairs* 9, no. 2 (1990), 4–5, http://content.healthaffairs.org/content/9/2/4.full.pdf+html;

5   Here is the raw data of a few dictionary definitions of the term *health*, and notice certain changes in the definition over the years, starting with the word's etymology (origin and influence from other languages).

Douglas Harper, *Online Etymological Dictionary*: "Old English *hælþ* 'wholeness, a being whole, sound or well,' from Proto-Germanic *hailitho*, from Proto-Indo-European *kailo-* 'whole, uninjured, of good omen' (cf. Old English *hal* 'hale, whole;' Old Norse *heill* 'healthy;' Old English *halig*, Old Norse *helge* 'holy, sacred;' Old English *hælan* 'to heal'). Of physical health in Middle English, but also 'prosperity, happiness, welfare; preservation, safety.'" S.v. "health," http://www.etymonline.com/index.php?term=health.

Noah Webster, *An American Dictionary of the English Language* (1828): "That state of an animal or living body, in which the parts are sound, well organized and disposed, and in which they all perform freely their natural functions. In this state the animal feels no pain. This word is applied also to plants.

1. Sound state of the mind; natural vigor of faculties.

2. Sound state of the mind, in a moral sense; purity; goodness.

There is no health in us.

3. Salvation or divine favor, or grace which cheers God's people. Ps.43,

4. Wish of health and happiness; used in drinking.

Come, love and health to all; an elliptical phrase, for, I wish health to you."

Note that the 1913 edition combines the first two senses of *health*, eliminates the third sense, and retains the fourth sense. To the revised first sense is appended "especially, the state of being free from physical disease or pain." S.v. "disease," http://www.1828-dictionary.com/d/search/word,disease.

Merriam-Webster Online Dictionary, (2012): "1a: the condition of being sound in body, mind, or spirit; especially: freedom from physical disease or pain b: the general condition of the body <in poor health> <enjoys good health>

2a: flourishing condition: well-being <defending the health of the beloved oceans —Peter Wilkinson> b: general condition or state <poor economic health>

3: a toast to someone's health or prosperity" S.v. "disease," http://www.merriam-webster.com/dictionary/health. Given these definitions, the World Health Organization's definition of *health* sounds good at first blush, except that it follows Webster's 1913 edition in eliminating the spiritual dimension of health, and is controversial for other reasons: "Health is a state of complete physical, mental, and social well-being and not merely the absence of disease or infirmity." "Definition of Health," World Health Organization, https://apps.who.int/aboutwho/en/definition.html. However, for an evaluation of this and various other definitions of *health*, see James A. Marcum and Robert B. Kruschwitz, "Revisioning Health," *Health* issue, *Christian Reflection: A Series in Faith and Ethics* (2007): 81–86, http://www.baylor.edu/christianethics/HealthArticleMarcumKruschwitz.pdf.

6 Here is the raw data of a few dictionary definitions of the term *disease*, and notice certain changes in the definition over the years, starting with the word's etymology (origin and influence from other languages).

7 Thomas L. Stedman, *Stedman's Medical Dictionary*, 26th ed. (Baltimore, MD: Williams & Wilkins, 1995), 764.

8 *Dorland's Medical Dictionary*, s.v. "disease," http://web.archive.org/web/20100411075617/http://www.mercksource.com/pp/us/cns/cns_hl_dorlands_split.jsp?pg=/ppdocs/us/common/dorlands/dorland/three/000030493.htm. For an exploration of the distinction between subjective and objective definitions of disease, see Lester S. King, "What Is Disease?" *Philosophy of Science* 21, no. 3 (1954):193–203. King defined disease as "the aggregate state of those conditions which, judged by the prevailing culture, are deemed painful or disabling, and which, at the same time, deviate from either the statistical norm or from some idealized status." His is kind of a "statistical" moving-target definition that can change with the prevailing moods of society. Theologically speaking, disease is much like sin in being a parasitic perversion of everything that is good, right, true, and beautiful in the human body.

9 Marcum and Kruschwitz, "Revisioning Health," 16–17.

10 Abigail Rian Evans, *Redeeming Marketplace Medicine: A Theology of Health Care* (Cleveland: Pilgrim Press, 1999; repr., Eugene, OR: Wipf & Stock, 2008), [PG. NO.???]

Chapter 1: We Are a Creation

11 George Alexander, "How Life on Earth Began," *Readers Digest*, November 1982, 116.

12 Jack W. Szostak, Martin M. Hanczyc, Irene A. Chen, Kourosh Salehi-Ashtiani, Michael Sacerdote, and Shelly Fujikawa, "Replicating Vesicles and the Origin of Life," abstract, in "Abstracts from the Astrobiology Science Conference 2004," supplement, *International Journal of Astrobiology* 3, no. S1 (2004): 1, doi: 10.1017/S14735500404001648.

13 Ibid., 2.

14 Amanda Bower, "Neurobiology: Mind Reader," *TIME* magazine, August 20, 2001, http://www.time.com/time/magazine/article/0,9171,1000599,00.html.

15 R Laird Harris, Gleason L. Archer Jr., and Bruce K. Waltke, *Theological Wordbook of the Old Testament*, (Chicago: Moody, 1980; electronic ed, 1999), 2:930.

16 Tim Challies, "Visual Theology: The Attributes of God" (image), http://s3.amazonaws.com/Challies_VisualTheology/the_attributes_of_God_hires.png; for more on the attributes of God, see *Theopedia: An Encyclopedia of Christianity*, s.v. "Attributes of God," "Classification of the Attributes of God," and "List of God's Known Attributes," http://www.theopedia.com/; also see the Westminster Shorter Catechism, Q&A 4: Q: What is God? A: God is a Spirit, infinite, eternal, and unchangeable, in his being, wisdom, power, holiness, justice, goodness, and truth.

17 As one biblical commentator has rendered 1 Corinthians 5:17: "So then, if any person [is] in Christ, new creation [becomes his perspective]. . . . the things of the old [order] have passed away; behold, the new [order] has come." Alternate translation provided by Carl B. Hoch Jr., *All Things New: The Significance of Newness for Biblical Theology* (Grand Rapids: Baker Book House, 1995), 160–61. The more familiar wording of the NIV and other versions is, "Therefore, if anyone is in Christ, he is a new creation; the old has gone, the new has come!"

18 E. W. Bullinger, *Number in Scripture: Its Supernatural Design and Spiritual Significance*, 4th ed. (1894; London:Eyre & Spottiswoode:

1921), 108, http://www.giveshare.org/library/numberscripture/index.html.

19   Norman L. Geisler and Frank Turek, *I Don't Have Enough Faith to Be an Atheist* (Wheaton: Crossway Books, 2004).

20   Charles Darwin to John Fordyce, 7 May 1879, Down Beckenham, Kent, transcribed by Darwin Correspondence Project, http://www.darwinproject.ac.uk/entry-12041, quoted in Augustus Hopkins Strong, *Systematic Theology*, Volume 1: *The Doctrine of God* (Philadelphia: Griffith & Rowland, 1907), 57. First published in 1886. Darwin closes the letter as follows: "I think that generally (& more and more so as I grow older) but not always, that an agnostic would be the most correct description of my state of mind."

21   C. S. Lewis, "Is Theology Poetry?" *Socratic Digest* 3 (1945), quoted in C. S. Lewis, *The Weight of Glory, and Other Addresses*, rev. ed., ed. Walter Hooper (1949; repr., New York: Macmillan, 1980), 140.

22   C. S. Lewis, *Surprised by Joy: The Shape of My Early Life* (1955; repr., New York, Harcourt Brace, 1995), 191.

23   Oswald Chambers, *God's Workmanship* (Hants, UK: Marshall, Morgan & Scott, 1953; electronic ed., 1996.

24   Ravi Zacharias, *The Real Face of Atheism* (Grand Rapids: Baker Books, 2004), 112.

25   Fred Hoyle, "Hoyle on Evolution," *Nature* 294, no. 5837 (November 12, 1981): 105.

26   "Gamete Fusion and the Prevention of Polyspermy" in S. F. Gilbert, *Developmental Biology*, 6th ed (Sunderland, MA: Sinauer Associates, 2000, http://www.ncbi.nlm.nih.gov/books/NBK10033/. For more information about the band of light that transverses the cell at the point of sperm entry, see references 77 (Steinhardt et al. 1977), 93 (Gilkey et al. 1978), and 184 (Hafner et al. 1988) at http://www.ncbi.nlm.nih.gov/books/NBK10093/.

Chapter 2: God's Purpose for Our Bodies

27   "Göbekli Tepe, Turkey, Overview," GHF Projects, Global Heritage Fund, http://globalheritagefund.org/what_we_do/overview/current_projects/gobekli_tepe_turkey.

28   Sandra Scham, "The World's First Temple," *Archaeology* 61, no. 6 (November/December 2008): http://www.archaeology.org/0811/abstracts/turkey.html.

29   Ibid.

30   In contrast and comparison to an evolutionary view of the world and its history, the Bible describes four biblical worlds in the course of its story: the first in Genesis 1–2 (the world God created good—paradise), the second in Genesis 3–7 (the world before the flood), the third in Genesis 8–Revelation 20 (our present post-flood world), and the fourth in Revelation 21 (the new world—new heaven and new earth). Old dates are notoriously difficult to get right or be sure of, but we can all agree that these artifacts and ruined temples were built and date back to a long time ago.

31   Ibid.

32   "Angkor Vat," Temples, APSARA, the Authority for the Protection and Management of Angkor and the Region of Siem Reap, http://www.autoriteapsara.org/en/angkor/temples_sites/temples/angkor_vat.html.

33   Thomas Cahill, *The Gifts of the Jews: How a Tribe of Desert Nomads Changed the Way Everyone Thinks and Feels* (New York: Nan A. Talese/Doubleday, Random House, 1998), 40–41. Cahill proceeds to detail the ancient belief and view of the cosmos in which originates the notion that the earth was a flat circle and heaven a sky dome under which hung the astral bodies portraying the drama of heaven, which was predictive of life on earth mirrored in its weakened form (41–42).

34   For a helpful survey of temple construction and its widely varying architecture from one religion to another, see *Encyclopædia Britannica Online*, s. v. "temple," http://www.britannica.com/EBchecked/topic/586791/temple (accessed August 16, 2012).

35   Paul David Tripp, *Instruments in the Redeemer's Hands: People in Need of Change Helping People in Need of Change* (Phillipsburg, NJ: P&R Publishing, 2002), 44.

36   The *Theological Wordbook of the Old Testament* defines this term as follows: "The noun *miqdāš* is used most frequently in the [Old Testament] as the designation of the tabernacle and the temple.

It is frequently translated 'sanctuary,' in these cases. In keeping with the basic meaning of the word group that it represents (*qdš*), *miqdāš* denotes that which has been devoted to the sphere of the sacred. When it refers to the sanctuary, it connotes the physical area devoted to the worship of God. This area was sacred because it was the place where God dwelled among the people (Ex 25:8) and its sanctity was not to be profaned (Lev 12:4; 19:30; 20:3; 21:12, 23)." R. Laird Harris, Gleason L. Archer Jr., and Bruce K. Waltke, *Theological Wordbook of the Old Testament*, (Chicago: Moody, 1980; electronic ed., 1999), 2:798.

37   For a newer study of the tabernacle, see David M. Levy, *The Tabernacle: Shadows of the Messiah; Its Sacrifices, Services, and Priesthood* (Bellmawr, NJ: Friends of Israel Gospel Ministry, 1993). For an older study of the tabernacle, see John Ritchie, *The Tabernacle in the Wilderness: A Study of Christ in the Tabernacle, the Offerings, and the Priesthood* (new ed., rev. and enl., Kilmarnock, Scotland: J. Ritchie, 1891; repr., Grand Rapids: Kregel, 1982). Originally published in 1884 by the Publishing Office in Glasgow.

38   For an up-to-date study of the temple, see Simon Goldhill, *The Temple of Jerusalem*, Wonders of the World (Cambridge, MA: Harvard University Press, 2005). With regard to the subject of this work, see especially chapter 6, "Your Body Is a Temple" (96–108) and corresponding bibliography for further reading (178–79).

39   Ibid., 7.

40   Michael E. Wittmer, *Heaven Is a Place on Earth: Why Everything You Do Matters to God* (Grand Rapids: Zondervan, 2004), 58.

41   Richard Wiseman, "New Year's Resolutions Experiment," Quirkology, http://www.quirkology.com/UK/Experiment_resolution.shtml.

42   *American Heritage Dictionary of the English Language*, 5th ed., s.v. "inspiration," http://ahdictionary.com/word/search. html?q=inspiration.

43   Ibid., s.v. "enthusiasm," http://ahdictionary.com/word/search. html?q=enthusiasm. The etymology or origin and development of the meaning of the word is traced as follows: "Late Latin *enthūsiasmus*, from Greek *enthousiasmos*, from *enthousiazein*, to be inspired by a god, from *entheos*, possessed : *en-*, in; see EN-[2] + *theos*,

god." See also *Etymological Dictionary Online*, s.v. "enthusiasm," http://www.etymonline.com/index.php?term=enthusiasm.

44   Oswald Chambers, *Jesus Wants All of Me*, adapted and illustrated Phil A Smouse (Grand Rapids: Promise Press, 1999). Based on the classic devotional *My Utmost for His Highest* by Oswald Chambers.

45   Robert Boyd Munger, *My Heart—Christ's Home*, rev. ed. (Downers Grove, IL: InterVarsity, 1986).

46   For more on the theology of human embodiment in the life to come, see Allison, "Toward a Theology of Human Embodiment," cited earlier, especially sections on "Death of the Body" (11–13) and "The Future of the Body" (13) as well as discussion in chapter 8, "Movement."

Chapter 3: Ruined Temples

47   Barry A. Kosmin and Ariela Keysar, *American Religious Identification Survey 2008*, Institute for the Study of Secularism in Society & Culture (Hartford, CT: 2008), http://b27.cc.trincoll.edu/weblogs/AmericanReligionSurvey-ARIS/reports/p1a_belong.html.

48   *The American Heritage New Dictionary of Cultural Literacy*, 3rd ed., Dictionary.com., s.v. "nihilism," http://dictionary.reference.com/browse/nihilism.

49   Peter A. Muennig and Sherry A. Glied, "What Changes in Survival Rates Tell Us about U.S. Health Care," *Health Affairs* (October 2010): 1, doi: 10.1377/hlthaff.2010.0073.

50   Goodarz Danaei, Eric L. Ding, Dariush Mozaffarian, Ben Taylor, Jürgen Rehm, Christopher J. L. Murray, Majid Ezzati, "The Preventable Causes of Death in the United States: Comparative Risk Assessment of Dietary, Lifestyle, and Metabolic Risk Factors" *PLoS Medicine* 6, no. 4 (2009): e1000058. doi:10.1371/journal.pmed.1000058.

51   Ibid.

52   Ibid.

53   Ibid.

54   Thomas Nordegren, *The A–Z Encyclopedia of Alcohol and Drug Abuse* (Parkland, FL: Brown Walker Press 2002), 37.

55   Centers for Disease Control and Prevention, "Youth Risk Behavior Surveillance—United States, 2009," Surveillance Summaries, June 5, 2010, *Morbidity and Mortality Weekly Report* 59, no. SS-5 (2010): 17, http://www.cdc.gov/mmwr/pdf/ss/ss5905.pdf.

56   "Misuse of Over-the-Counter Cough and Cold Medications among Persons Aged 12 to 25," *The National Survey on Drug Use and Health Report* (Rockville, MD: Substance Abuse and Mental Health Services Administration, 2008), http://www.oas.samhsa.gov/2k8/cough/cough.htm.

57   National Data, The National Campaign to Prevent Teen and Unplanned Pregnancy, www.thenationalcampaign.org/national-data/default.aspx.

58   Leadership Survey, *Christianity Today*, December 2001; Pornography, Quick Facts, Ethics and Religious Liberty Commission of the Southern Baptist Commission, http://erlc.com/issues/quick-facts/por/; Men—Stats, XXXChurch.com, http://www.xxxchurch.com/men/stats.html.

59   Adultery: Just the Statistics, KellyBonewell.com, January 21, 2011, www.kellybonewell.com/psychology/adultery-just-the-statistics/.

60   Melisa Steele, "National Statistics for Anorexia with Anorexia Charts: The Slow Suicide," Teen Beauty Tips, www.teen-beauty-tips.com/national-statistics-for-anorexia.html.

61   Arthur C. Guyton and John E. Hall, *Guyton and Hall Textbook of Medical Physiology*, 12th ed. (Philadelphia: Saunders: 2011): 9.

62   For a thoroughgoing study that will stimulate much thought toward helping us envision what a church that delivers holistic health care could look like, see Abigail Rian Evans, *The Healing Church: Practical Programs for Health Ministries* (Cleveland: United Church Press, 1999). For a blog post on parish nursing, see Maria Peace, "Parish Nursing," *ubfriends.org*, May 22, 2012, http://www.ubfriends.org/2012/05/22/parish-nursing-2/.

63   Wendell Berry, "Health Is Membership" in *The Art of the Commonplace: Agrarian Essays of Wendell Berry*, ed. Norman Wirzba (Washington, DC: Counterpoint, 2002), 144, 146.

64   For passages that discuss God's temple as his house, see 2 Samuel 7 and 1 Chronicles 29.

Chapter 4: Generations

65   Olshansky et al., "Potential Decline in Life Expectancy," 352.

66   Peter Sterling, "Principles of Allostasis: Optimal Design, Predictive Regulation, Pathophysiology, and Rational Therapeutics," in Jay Schulkin, ed., *Allostasis, Homeostasis, and the Cost of Physiological Adaptation* (New York: Cambridge University Press, 2004), 41.

67   Danaei et al., "Preventable Causes of Death in the United States," e1000058.

68   Tapio Videman, "Experimental Models of Osteoarthritis: The Role of Immobilization," *Clinical Biomechanics* 2, no. 4 *(1987)*: 223–29.

69   Danaei et al., "Preventable Causes of Death in the United States," e1000058.

Chapter 5: Boundaries

70   *American Heritage Dictionary of the English Language*, 5th ed., s.v. "boundaries," http://ahdictionary.com/word/search.html?q=boundary.

71   *Merriam-Webster* OnLine, s.v., "gluttony," http://www.merriam-webster.com/dictionary/gluttony.

Chapter 6: The Mind

72   Rick Renner, *Sparkling Gems from the Greek: 365 Greek Word Studies for Every Day of the Year to Sharpen Your Understanding of God's Word* (Tulsa, OK: Teach All Nations 2003), 2.

73   Joe E. Holoubek and Alice B. Holoubek, "Blood, Sweat, and Fear: 'A Classification of Hematidrosis'" *Journal of Medicine* 27 nos., 3–4 (1996): 115–33, http://www.ncbi.nlm.nih.gov/pubmed/8982961.

74   Ibid.

75   Dorthe Kirkegaard Thomsen, Mimi Yung Mehlsen, Marianne Hokland, Andrus Viidik, Frede Olesen, Kirsten Avlund, Karen Munk, and Robert Zachariae, "Negative Thoughts and Health: Associations among Rumination, Immunity, and Health Care Utilization in a Young and Elderly Sample," *Psychosomatic Medicine* 66, no. 3 (2004): 363–71, doi:10.1097/01.psy.0000127688.44363.fb.

76 Shuhei Izawa, Urara Hirata, Masahisa Kodama, Shinobu Nomura, "Effect of Hostility on Salivary Cortisol Levels in University Students" [article in Japanese], *Shinrigaku Kenkyu* 78, no. 3 (2007): 277–83, http://www.ncbi.nlm.nih.gov/pubmed/17892025.

77 Robert M. Sapolsky, *Why Zebra Don't Get Ulcers*, (New York: W. H. Freeman and Company, 1998), 2–3.

78 Ralph E. Parchment, Donna A. Volpe, Patricia M. LoRusso, Connie L. Erickson-Miller, Martin J. Murphy Jr., and Charles K. Grieshaber, "In Vivo-In Vitro Correlation of Myelotoxicity of 9-Methoxypyrazoloacridine [NSC-366140, PD115934] to Myeloid and Erythroid Hematopoietic Progenitors from Human, Murine, and Canine Marrow," *Journal of the National Cancer Institute* 86, no. 4 (1994): 256–57, doi: 10.1093/jnci/86.4.273; Marty S. Player, Dana E. King, Arch G. Mainous III, and Mark E. Geesey, "Psychosocial Factors and Progression from Prehypertension to Hypertension or Coronary Heart Disease," *Annals of Family Medicine* 5, no. 5 (2007): 403–11, doi: 10.1370/afm.738; Izawa et al., "Effect of Hostility on Salivary Cortisol Levels," 277–83.

79 Erik J. Giltay, Marjolein H. Kamphuis, Sandra Kalmijn, Frans G. Zitman, Daan Kromhout, "Dispositional Optimism and the Risk of Cardiovascular Death: The Zutphen Elderly Study," *Archives of Internal Medicine* 166, no. 4, (2006): 431–36, doi:10.1001/archinte.166.4.431; Matthew C. Whited, Amanda L. Wheat, and Kevin T. Larkin, "The Influence of Forgiveness and Apology on Cardiovascular Reactivity and Recovery in Response to Mental Stress," *Journal of Behavioral Medicine* 33, no. 4 (2010): 293, doi: 10.1007/s10865-010-9259-7.

80 Parchment et al., "In Vivo-In Vitro Correlation of Myelotoxicity of 9-Methoxypyrazoloacridine," 256–57.

81 Takashi Hayashi, Satoru Tsujii, Tadao Iburi, Tamiko Tamanaha, Keiko Yamagami, Rieko Ishibashi, Miyo Hori, Shigeko Sakamoto, Hiroshi Ishii, Kazuo Murakami, "Laughter Up-regulates the Genes Related to NK Cell Activity in Diabetes," *Biomedical Research* 28, no. 6 (2007): 281–85.

82 David L. Jeffrey, *A Dictionary of Biblical Tradition in English Literature* (Grand Rapids: Eerdmans, 1992), s.v. "Sword of the Spirit."

83   Tony Evans, "'The Sword of the Spirit,' Ephesians 6:10–17," The Armor of God (sermon, Oak Cliff Bible Fellowship, Dallas, Texas, July 10, 2010), Digging Deeper, The Urban Alternative, http://www.loisevans.org/site/c.nkI2KhMWItF/b.6161337/k.DF22/Reading_Rm__Pg103__TE__The_Sword_of_the_Spirit__wk_93.htm.

Chapter 7: Emptiness on a Full Stomach

84   Kathleen DesMaisons, *Potatoes Not Prozac: Simple Solutions for Sugar Sensitivity* (New York: Simon & Schuster, 2008), 76–78.

85   Elliott M. Blass and Lisa B. Watt, "Suckling- and Sucrose-induced Analgesia in Human Newborns," *Pain* 83, no. 3 (1999): 611–23, doi:10.1016/S0304-3959(99)00166-9; Elliott M. Blass and Atish Shah, "Pain-reducing Properties of Sucrose in Human Newborns," *Chemical Senses* 20, no. 1 (1995): 29–35, doi:10.1093/chemse/20.1.29; Elliott Blass, Eileen Fitzgerald, and Priscilla Kehoe, "Interactions between Sucrose, Pain and Isolation Distress," *Pharmacology Biochemistry and Behavior* 26, no. 3 (1987): 483–89, doi:10.1016/0091-3057(87)90153-5; Elliott M. Blass, Thomas J. Fillion, Aron Weller, and Liesette Brunson, "Separation of Opioid from Nonopioid Mediation of Affect in Neonatal Rats: Nonopioid Mechanisms Mediate Maternal Contact Influences," *Behavioral Neuroscience* 104, no. 4 (1990): 625–36, doi: 10.1037/0735-7044.104.4.625.

86   Classical conditioning is usually done by pairing the two stimuli, as in Pavlov's classic experiments. Pavlov presented dogs with a ringing bell (conditioned stimulus) followed by food (unconditioned stimulus). The food (unconditioned stimulus) elicited salivation (unconditioned response), and after repeated bell-food pairings the bell also caused the dogs to salivate (conditioned response).

87   Sterling, "Principles of Allostasis" in Schulkin, *Allostasis, Homeostasis, and the Cost of Physiological Adaptation*, 47.

88   Richard J. Wurtman and Judith J. Wurtman, "Carbohydrates and Depression" *Scientific American* 260 (January 1989): 68–75, http://wurtmanlab.mit.edu/static/pdf/649.pdf.

89   Candace B. Pert, *Molecules of Emotion: Why You Feel the Way You Feel* (New York: Scribner: 1997), 298.

90   Magalie Lenoir, Fuschia Serre, Lauriane Cantin, Serge H. Ahmed, "Intense Sweetness Surpasses Cocaine Reward," *PLoS ONE* 2, no. 8 (2007): e698, doi:10.1371/journal.pone.0000698.

91   Christopher J. Ferguson, Monica E. Muñoz, and Maria R. Medrano, "Advertising Influences on Young Children's Food Choices and Parental Influence," *Journal of Pediatrics* 160, no. 3 (2012): 452–55, doi:10.1016/j.jpeds.2011.08.023.

92   Vinay Kumar, Abul K. Abbas, and Stanley L. Robbins, *Robbins Basic Pathology*, 9th ed. (Philadelphia: Elsevier Saunders, 2013), 7.

93   Diane Mapes, "Praise the Lard? Religion Linked to Obesity in Young Adults," MSNBC.com, updated March 25, 2011, http://www.msnbc. msn.com/id/42256829/ns/health-diet_and_nutrition/t/praise-lard-religion-linked-obesity-young-adults/#.UBiVuaN8TO5.

94   Sometimes it's instructive to look up where a word such as *disease* comes from and check out a much older definition and compare it to today's dictionaries. A shift from "cause" to "condition" is one difference from an older to a newer definition.

Douglas Harper, *Online Etymological Dictionary*: "early 14th century, 'discomfort, inconvenience,' from Old French *desaise* 'lack, want; discomfort, distress; trouble, misfortune; disease, sickness,' from *des-* 'without, away' (see *dis-*) + *aise* 'ease' (see *ease*). Sense of 'sickness, illness' in English first recorded late 14th century; the word still sometimes was used in its literal sense early 17th century." S.v. "disease," http://www.etymonline.com/index. php?term=disease.

Noah Webster, *An American Dictionary of the English Language* (1828): "The cause of pain or uneasiness; distemper; malady; sickness; disorder; any state of a living body in which the natural functions of the organs are interrupted or disturbed, either by defective or preternatural action, without a disrupture of parts by violence, which is called a wound. The first effect of disease is uneasiness or pain, and the ultimate effect is death. A disease may affect the whole body, or a particular limb or part of the body. We say a diseased limb; a disease in the head or stomach; and such partial affection of the body is called a local or topical disease. The word is also applied to the disorders of other animals, as well as to those of man; and to any derangement of the vegetative functions of plants." S.v. "disease," http://www.1828-dictionary.com/d/search/word,disease.

Merriam-Webster Online Dictionary, (2012): "a condition of the living animal or plant body or of one of its parts that impairs normal functioning and is typically manifested by distinguishing signs and symptoms: sickness, malady." S.v. "disease," http://www.merriam-webster.com/dictionary/disease.

95 James M. Grier, *The Ten Words: Moral Choices Begin with the Ten Commandments*, Lesson 1, Thursday Evening Bible Class, Fall 1991, Grand Rapids Baptist Seminary, MP3 audio file, http://jamesmgrier.org/audiofiles/10%20Words%20Lesson%202.mp3.

96 *Dictionary.com Unabridged*, s.v. "glutton," http://dictionary.reference.com/browse/glutton.

97 *American Heritage Dictionary of the English Language*, 5th ed., s.v. "integrity," http://ahdictionary.com/word/search.html?q=integrity.

98 Michael Pollen, "Unhappy Meals," *New York Times* Magazine, January 28, 2007, http://www.nytimes.com/2007/01/28/magazine/28nutritionism.t.html; Michael Pollen, *In Defense of Food: An Eater's Manifesto* (New York: Penguin Press, 2008), 1.

Chapter 8: Movement

99 Jeffrey, S. Bland, "Rhythmic Aspects of Functional Medical Therapies," (presentation, Sixth International Symposium on Functional Medicine, Tucson, Arizona, May 24, 1999).

100 Daniel M. Landers, *The Influence of Exercise on Mental Health*, Research Digest 2, no. 12 (Washington, DC: President's Council on Physical Fitness and Sports, 1997).

101 James A. Blumenthal, Michael A. Babyak, Kathleen A. Moore, W. Edward Craighead, Steve Herman, Parinda Khatri, Robert Waugh, et al., "Effects of Exercise Training on Older Patients with Major Depression," *Archives of Internal Medicine* 159, no. 19 (October 25, 1999): 2349–56, doi: 10-1001/pubs.Arch Intern Med.-ISSN-0003-9926-159-19-ioi81361; James A. Blumenthal, Michael A. Babyak, P. Murali Doraiswamy, Lana Watkins, Benson M. Hoffman, Krista A. Barbour, Steve Herman, et al., "Exercise and Pharmacotherapy

in the Treatment of Major Depressive Disorder," *Psychosomatic Medicine* 69, no. 7 (September 2007): 587–96, doi: 10.1097/PSY.0b013e318148c19a; Andrea L. Dunn, Madhukar H. Trivedi, James B. Kampert, Camillia G. Clark, and Heather O. Chambliss, "Exercise Treatment for Depression: Efficacy and Dose Response," *American Journal of Preventive Medicine* 28, no. 1 (January 2005): 1–8, doi: 10.1016/j.amepre.2004.09.003.

102   K. R. Fox, "The Influence of Physical Activity on Mental Well-Being," *Public Health Nutrition* 2, no. 3a (1999): 411–18; Carl W. Cotman, Nicole C. Berchtold, Lori-Ann Christie, "Exercise Builds Brain Health: Key Roles of Growth Factor Cascades and Inflammation," *Trends in Neurosciences*, 30, no. 10, (October 2007), 464–72, doi: 10.1016/j.tins.2007.06.011; C. C. Streeter, J. E. Jensen, R. M. Perlmutter, H. J. Cabral, H. Tian, D. B. Terhune, D. A. Ciraulo, P. F. Renshaw, "Yoga Asana Sessions Increase Brain GABA Levels: A Pilot Study," *Journal of Alternate and Complementary Medicine* 13, no. 4 (2007): 419–26, doi: 10.1089/acm.2007.6338.

103   Christian K. Roberts and R. James Barnard, "Effects of Exercise and Diet on Chronic Disease," *Journal of Applied Physiology* 2005:98 3-30, doi: 10.1152/japplphysiol.00852.2004; *American Journal of Clinical Nutrition* (2004). AUTHOR(S), "ARTICLE TITLE," *American Journal of Clinical Nutrition* [vol. no.], no. [issue no.] (2004): PAGES.

104   John H. Weisburger, "Vitamin C in Disease Prevention," *Journal of the American College of Nutrition* 14, no. 2 (1995): 109–11.

105   AUTHOR(S), "ARTICLE TITLE," *Physician and Sportsmedicine* 21, no. 1 (January 1993): 125–33.

106   L. B. Borghouts and H. A. Keizer, "Exercise and Insulin Sensitivity: A Review," *International Journal of Sports Medicine* 21, no. 1 (2000): 1–12.

107   R. L. Swezey, "Exercise for Osteoporosis—Is Walking Enough? The Case for Site Specificity and Resistive Exercise," *Spine* 21 (1996): 2809–13.

108   Mike Evans, "23 and 1/2 hours: What Is the Single Best Thing We Can Do for Our Health?" March 9, 2012, *My Favorite Medicine*, http://www.myfavouritemedicine.com/23-and-a-half-hours/. See

below on webpage for list of key references on which the video presentation is based.

109 Allison, "Toward a Theology of Human Embodiment," 13.

110 For more on an embodied alternative to the Gnostic understanding of the Christian life and the redemption of modern medicine, Joel Shuman and Brian Volck, *Reclaiming the Body: Christians and the Faithful Use of Modern Medicine*, Christian Practice of Everyday Life (Grand Rapids: Brazos, 2006); Jean Denton, ed., *Good Is the Flesh: Body, Soul, and Christian Faith* (Harrisburg, PA: Morehouse, 2005). For a review of these books, see Keith G. Meador, "Redeeming Medicine," review of *Reclaiming the Body: Christians and the Faithful Use of Modern Medicine* by Joel Shuman and Brian Volck, and *Good Is the Flesh: Body, Soul, and Christian Faith* edited by Jean Denton, Health issue, *Christian Reflection: A Series in Faith and Ethics* (2007), http://www.baylor.edu/christianethics/HealthReviewMeador.pdf.

111 James M. Grier, "Reproductive Technologies," (lecture, Bioethics & the Bible, College Park Church, Indianapolis, Indiana, April 19, 2008), MP3 audio file, http://jamesmgrier.org/audiofiles/BioEthics_Session2.mp3; PDF file, http://jamesmgrier.org/wp-content/uploads/2008/06/college-park-reproductive-tech.pdf. This idea was presented in the context of bioethics and applied to infertility and childlessness but in principle extends outward and includes other physical evils as well.

112 Jeffrey H. Boyd, *Being Sick Well: Joyful Living Despite Chronic Illness* (Grand Rapids: Baker Books, 2005). Also see Wendy Drew Wallace, *Doing Well at Being Sick: Living with Chronic and Acute Illness* (Grand Rapids: Discovery House Publishers, 2010).

Chapter 9: The Bottom Line

113 Graham Kendrick, "Meekness and Majesty (This Is Your God)," *Make Way for the King of Kings: A Carnival of Praise* (Make Way Music/Kingsway Music Ltd, 1986), http://www.grahamkendrick.co.uk/songs/lyrics/meekness.php. See Luke 2:7; John 1:14; and Colossins 2:9.

114 James Morgante, "Toward a Theology of Wellness," *Health Progress* (November–December 2002), 24, http://www.chausa.

Notes

org/authorindex.aspx?year=2002. For more on the integration of contemporary and holistic medicine from a Catholic perspective, including holistic thinking within the health care system, see also James Morgante, "An Argument Against the Use of the Term Spiritual Care," *Vision* (July 2002), http://www.nacc.org/vision/articles/term-spiritual-care.asp.

115 Morgante, "Toward a Theology of Wellness," 25.

116 Tony Evans, "Discovering the Strength of Faith," Comforting the Afflicted (sermon, Oak Cliff Bible Fellowship, Dallas, Texas, August 12, 2012), *The Alternative*, http://www.oneplace.com/ministries/the-alternative/listen/the-alternative-287879.html.

117 *Merriam-Webster* OnLine, s.v., "accountability," http://www.merriam-webster.com/dictionary/accountability.

118 For more on the intersection of health and Christian ethics, see the *Health* issue of *Christian Reflection: A Series in Faith and Ethics* 16 (2007), published by the Center for Christian Ethics at Baylor University, http://www.baylor.edu/christianethics/Health.pdf; e.g., see Mary Louise Bringle, "Eating Well: Seven Paradoxes of Plenty," *Health* issue, *Christian Reflection* 16 (2007): 27–34, http://www.baylor.edu/christianethics/HealthArticleBringle.pdf.

For more on the intersection of food and Christian ethics, see the *Food and Hunger* issue of *Christian Reflection: A Series in Faith and Ethics* 13 (Fall 2004), published by the Center for Christian Ethics at Baylor University, http://www.baylor.edu/christianethics/FoodandHunger.pdf; e.g., see Thomas Hibbs, "Hungry Souls," *Food and Hunger* issue, *Christian Reflection* 13 (Fall 2004): 18–25; Lori Brand Bateman, "We Are *How* We Eat," *Food and Hunger* issue, *Christian Reflection* 13 (Fall 2004): 89–93.

For a more environmentally focused article, see Nathan Bechtold, "Eating God's Way," *Relevant* (August 24, 2011), http://www.relevantmagazine.com/god/mission/features/26568-eating-gods-way.

About the Author

D r. **Ryan Bentley** has been described as one of the brightest young leaders in the field of nutritional medicine. A true innovator, Dr. Bentley has emerged on the national scene in natural medicine circles with his engaging seminars and the release of his book *Sex, Lies, and Cholesterol*, which is being praised by practitioners and laypeople alike.

As a child Dr. Bentley always aspired to become a doctor. From a young age he would read about childbirth in an encyclopedia, while sitting under the shopping cart at the local grocery store while his mother shopped. As time progressed he found himself immersed in athletics and weight training. It was during this time that he became strongly interested in enhancing his body's physiology to improve his athletic performance. Dr. Bentley went on to play college football at the University of Evansville. It was there at Evansville that Dr. Bentley saw the "flash of light" that occurs at the moment life is conceived (see chapter 1). His astonishment at the divine creation of human beings and his then recent acceptance of

Jesus Christ as his Lord and Savior sparked a fire in him to fulfill his childhood passion to become a doctor. Dr. Bentley decided to give up football and his social life to enroll at Indiana University and study biology in order to finish the requirements for medical school.

It was during his study at Indiana University that Dr. Bentley first realized that the human body was designed to be a self-healing and self-regulating system, provided there were sufficient nutrients available and an environment void of toxicities. While at Indiana University he participated in an experiment, through IU Medical School, that studied the effects of hormone replacement therapy. To his amazement, the drug studied was approved for use and was being taken by millions of women, yet it caused cancer in approximately 75 percent of the animals studied, as compared to the control group. It was at this time that Dr. Bentley struggled with a moral dilemma, as his medical education would be highly dependent upon administering approved drugs to suppress symptoms—drugs that often lead to side effects while frequently failing to treat the root cause of the symptoms.

He then decided to entertain the thought of becoming an orthopedic surgeon or emergency room physician. Dr. Bentley shadowed a number of doctors in the respective disciplines but was still unsure of his direction. During this time an old football injury in his lower back flared up, causing him to seek help. Previous to this episode he had been told by his college team physician that he would need rods and screws put into his lower back, but Dr. Bentley opted to "tough it out" when he was told that he would likely have a hard time doing things like playing with his future children or being athletic. Thus, for him surgery was not going to be an option.

Desperate and lacking options, while in much pain, Dr. Bentley stopped by an office where there was a doctor of chiropractic on staff. This office visit changed his life forever. In a matter of thirty seconds Dr. Bentley found himself pain free. He thought to himself, *No drugs! No surgery! No more pain! What is this profession all about?* Dr. Bentley then found himself shadowing a number of doctors of chiropractic. When he realized that he could do all the things he aspired to do in caring for the human body without facing a personal moral dilemma, he then applied for admittance to National University of Health Sciences. He has never looked back.

Dr. Bentley received his first bachelor's degree in biology from Indiana University, and while at National University of Health Sciences he also received his second bachelor's degree in human biology, while completing two fellowships in the Department of Anatomy before earning his Doctorate of Chiropractic, graduating cum laude.

Dr. Bentley also taught at the College of Dupage as an anatomy and physiology professor while in school. It was during his time at National University of Health Sciences that Dr. Bentley and his wife had two babies that did not make it to term; they were devastated and had no answers as to why. However, it was these events that catapulted their lives into an understanding of what it means to walk by faith. Determined to have a family, Dr. Bentley engrossed himself into a deeper understanding of human physiology in an effort to better understand cause and effect. At this point he started to master the interconnectedness of the human body and its interactions, both internally and externally. It is through his faith, study, and persistence to seek truth that he is able today to enjoy spending time not only with his amazing wife but also with their three miraculous children.

He has dedicated his personal and professional life to providing the truth that he has learned with regard to health, healing, and faith both to physicians and to the general public. Dr. Bentley takes pleasure in speaking nationally, helping patients, researching, studying truth, and writing.

Dr. Bentley is the cofounder and CEO of *The Wellness Prescription and BIA Education*, two companies created to educate practitioners on how to construct proven, objective, and quantifiable systems and protocols to help their patients reach optimal health. He has taught his principled nutritional approach to thousands of doctors around the country.

Dr. Bentley and his family live in Holland, Michigan.

Bonus Online Resources

I trust that the book **Vessels that Thrive** will help you as you consider the many facets involved in choosing a lifestyle of health, healing, and faith. Yet there is only so much that can be said in a book. I have a lot more to share about achieving health while living out your purpose, so together we're going to keep the conversation going. Look for user-friendly bonus resources online to help you in your journey of becoming a **vessel that thrives**. Visit the book website *www.vesselsthatthrive. com* to check out what's new.

If you are inspired to become a **vessel that thrives** and to live life as God intended but would like some specific additional guidance, I have created complimentary Life Application Manuals as supplemental health resources for you. These **FREE** additional resources include:

- "Achieving Mindful Peace"
- "Thrive on Live Food Guide"
- "Made to Move Exercise Guide"

To access this free bonus material that extends certain aspects of **Vessels that Thrive**, go now to *www.vesselsthatthrive.com/ bookbonus* and enter your name and email.

If you would like to request Dr. Ryan Bentley for a speaking engagement at your church or conference event or to hold a biblical health seminar, please send an email to *info@vesselsthatthrive.com.*